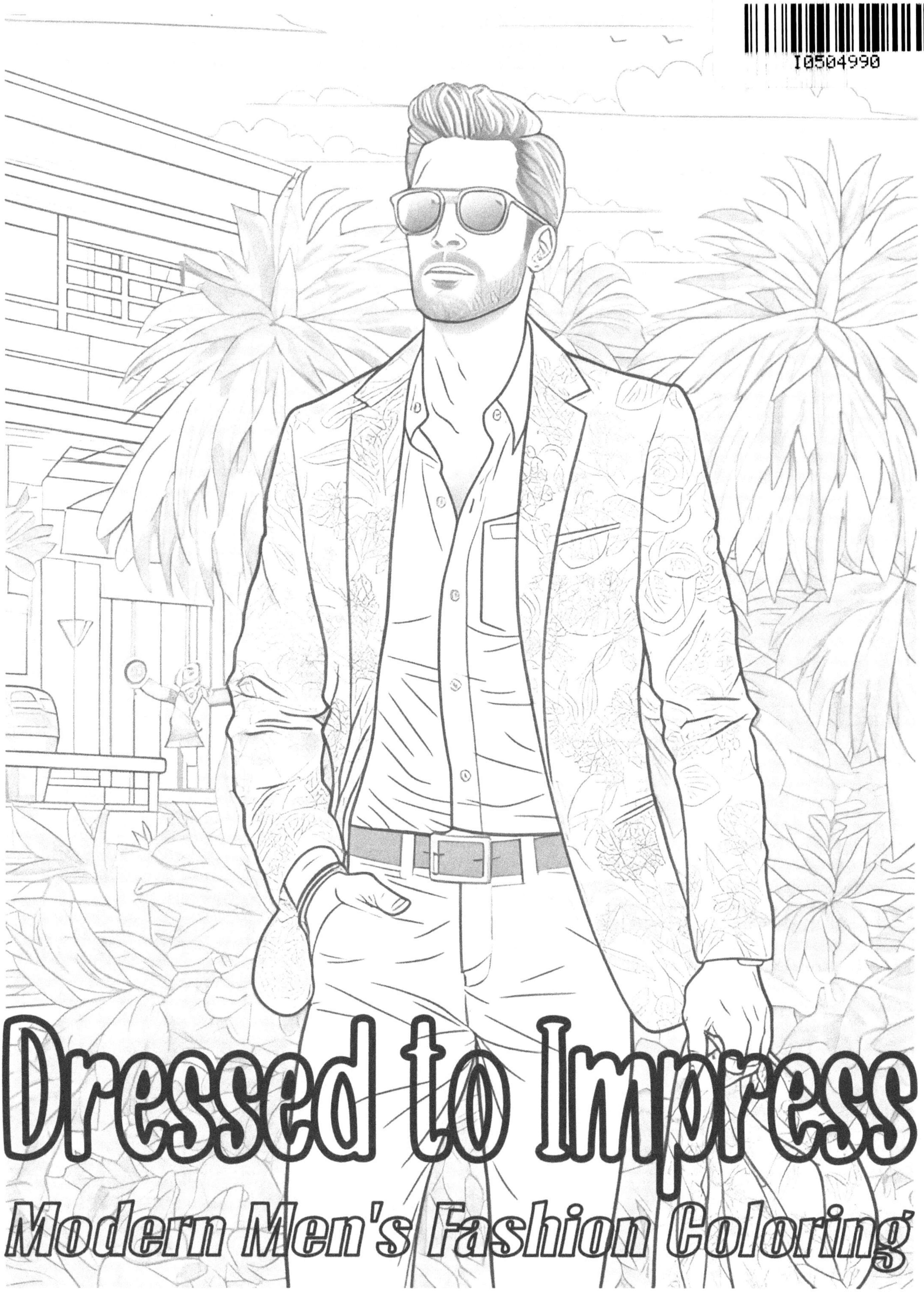

Dressed to Impress

Modern Men's Fashion Coloring

This book belong to

_____

_____

Preface

Welcome to "Dressed to Impress: Modern Men's Fashion Coloring"! Within the pages of this coloring book, you will embark on a creative journey that celebrates the vibrant world of men's fashion and style. Prepare to immerse yourself in a tapestry of modern sartorial elegance, where every stroke of color will breathe life into the captivating ensembles of contemporary gentlemen.

Fashion is not merely an expression of personal style; it is an art form that allows individuals to convey their unique identities and make a statement without uttering a word. In this coloring book, we delve into the ever-evolving realm of men's fashion, exploring a myriad of styles, trends, and themes that define the modern man's wardrobe.

From classic suits and streetwear swagger to avant-garde couture and casual denim looks, "Dressed to Impress" showcases a diverse range of fashion choices, enabling you to unleash your creativity and infuse each page with your own artistic vision. Every illustration is meticulously crafted to capture the essence of contemporary men's style, with attention to detail that reflects the intricate craftsmanship found in the world of fashion design.

As you embark on this coloring adventure, feel free to experiment with colors, patterns, and textures, and make each illustration a reflection of your personal aesthetic. Whether you prefer bold and vibrant hues, subtle and muted tones, or an eclectic mix of shades, this book invites you to unleash your imagination and bring these stylish men's outfits to life.

Moreover, "Dressed to Impress" serves as a source of inspiration, allowing you to explore various fashion themes and discover new trends. It encourages you to delve into the world of fashion and develop an appreciation for the artistry and creativity behind every stitch and fabric choice.

So, grab your coloring tools and get ready to embark on a captivating journey through the realms of modern men's fashion. Let your brushes and pencils be your guide as you paint each page with your unique interpretation of style. Get ready to immerse yourself in a world where elegance, confidence, and creativity blend harmoniously.

Remember, in this book, you are not just a colorist but a fashion artist. Let your artistic flair soar as you fill these pages with vibrant shades, bringing these stylish men to life in a kaleidoscope of colors. Whether you choose to reimagine established trends or create your own, let your coloring journey be a testament to the limitless possibilities of fashion.

Now, let us embark together on this artistic voyage, where fashion and creativity intertwine, and where every stroke of color brings us closer to capturing the essence of modern men's style. Let "Dressed to Impress: Modern Men's Fashion Coloring" be your canvas, and may your journey be a truly inspiring and colorful one.

Happy coloring!

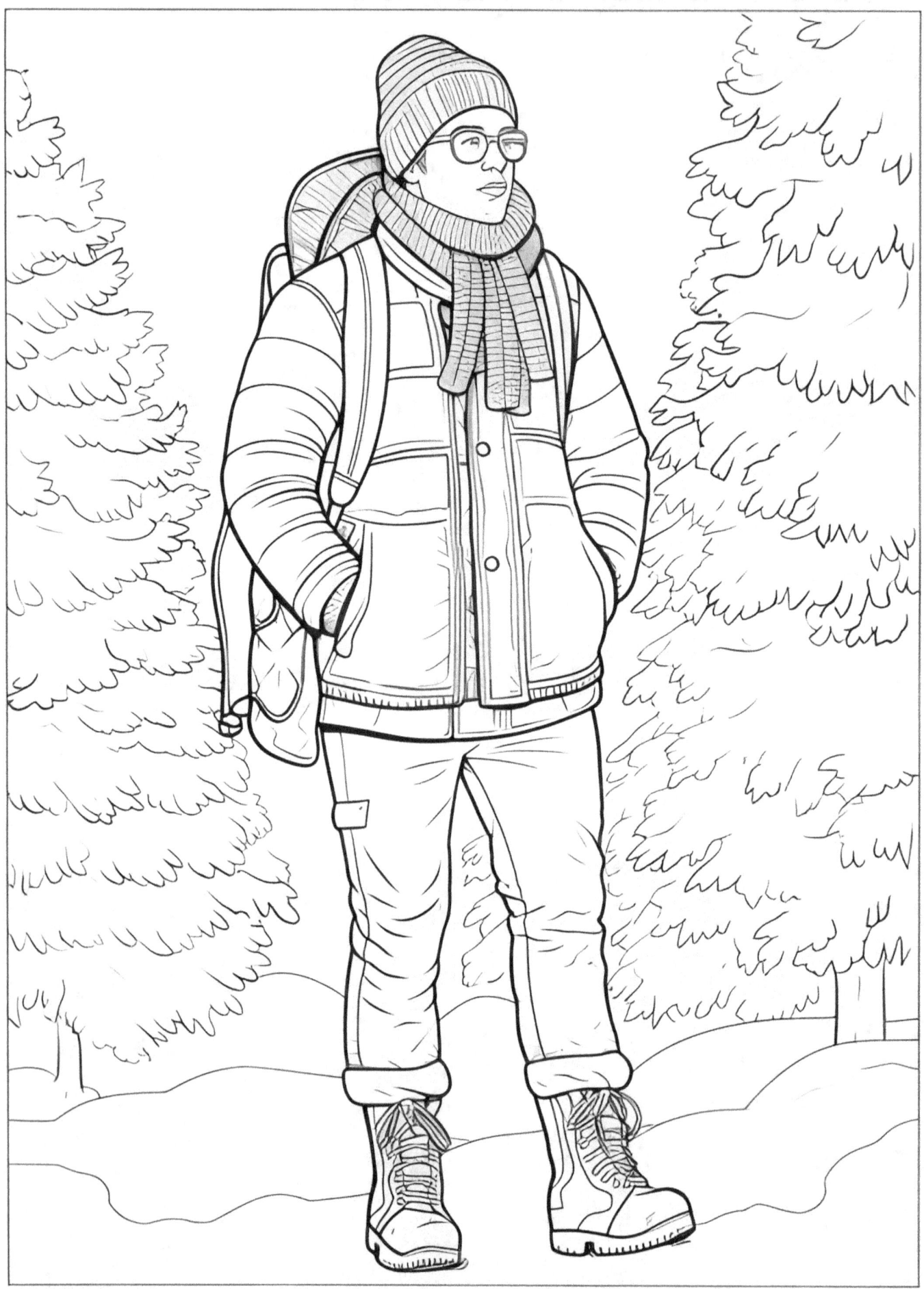

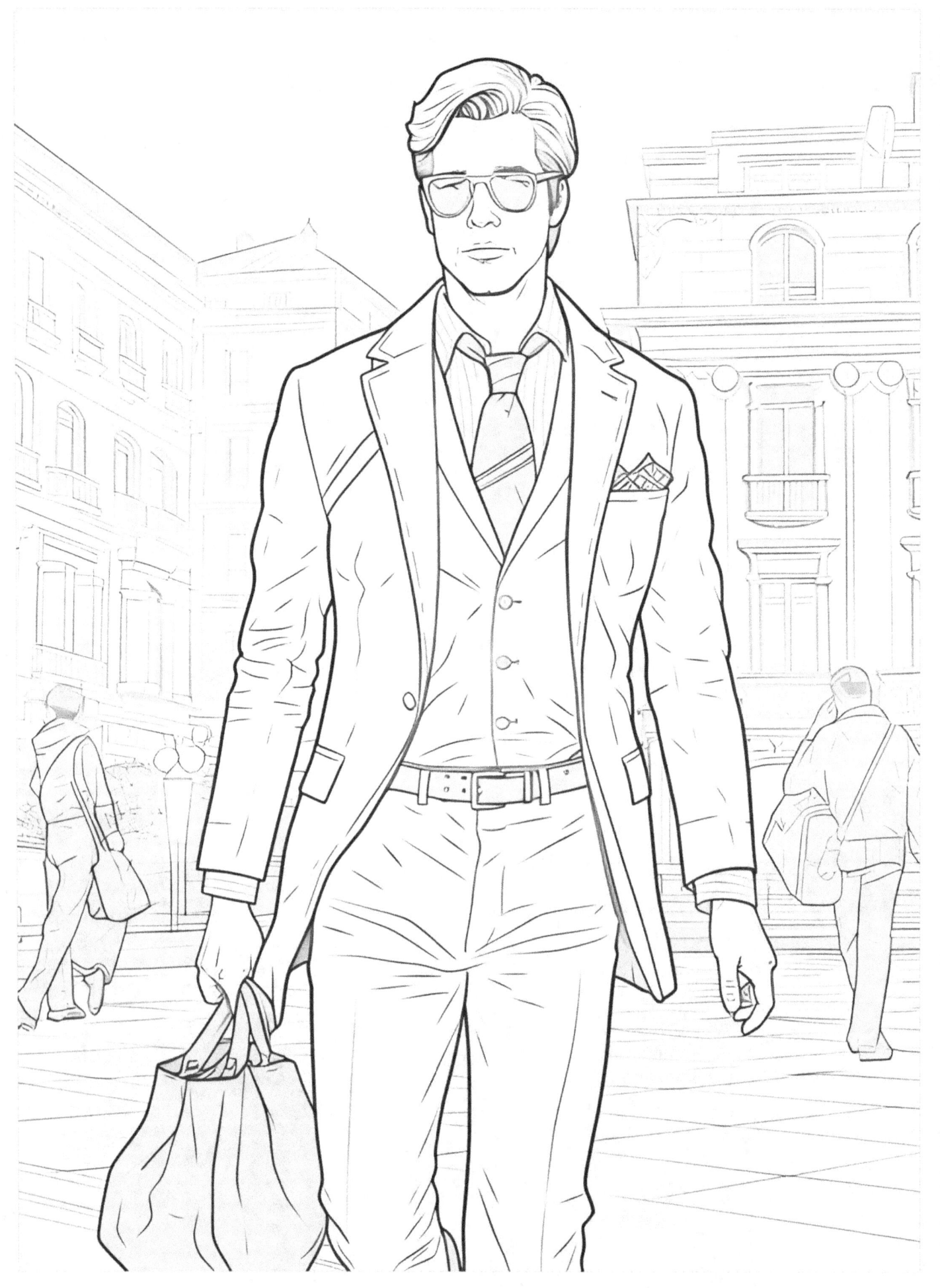

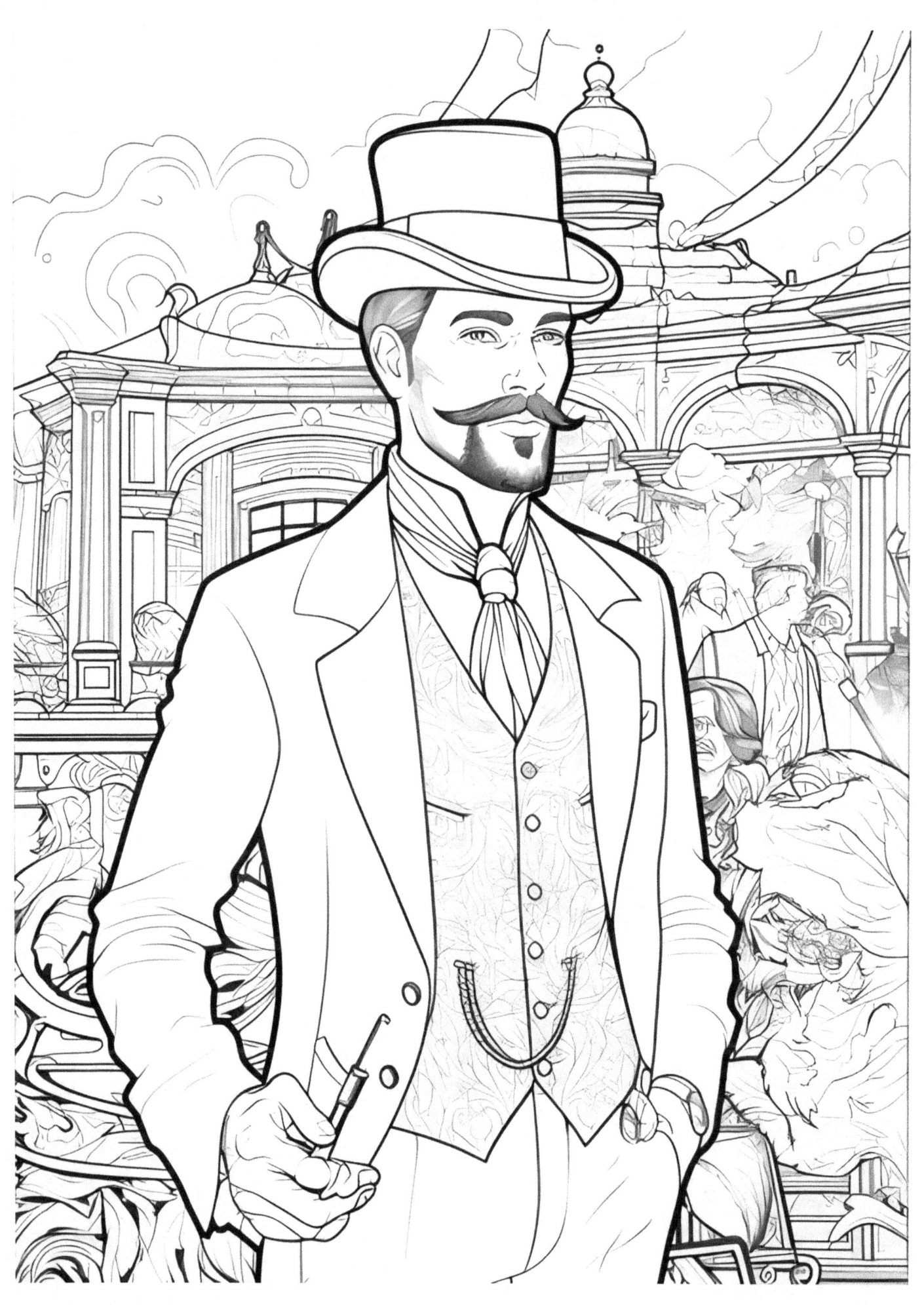

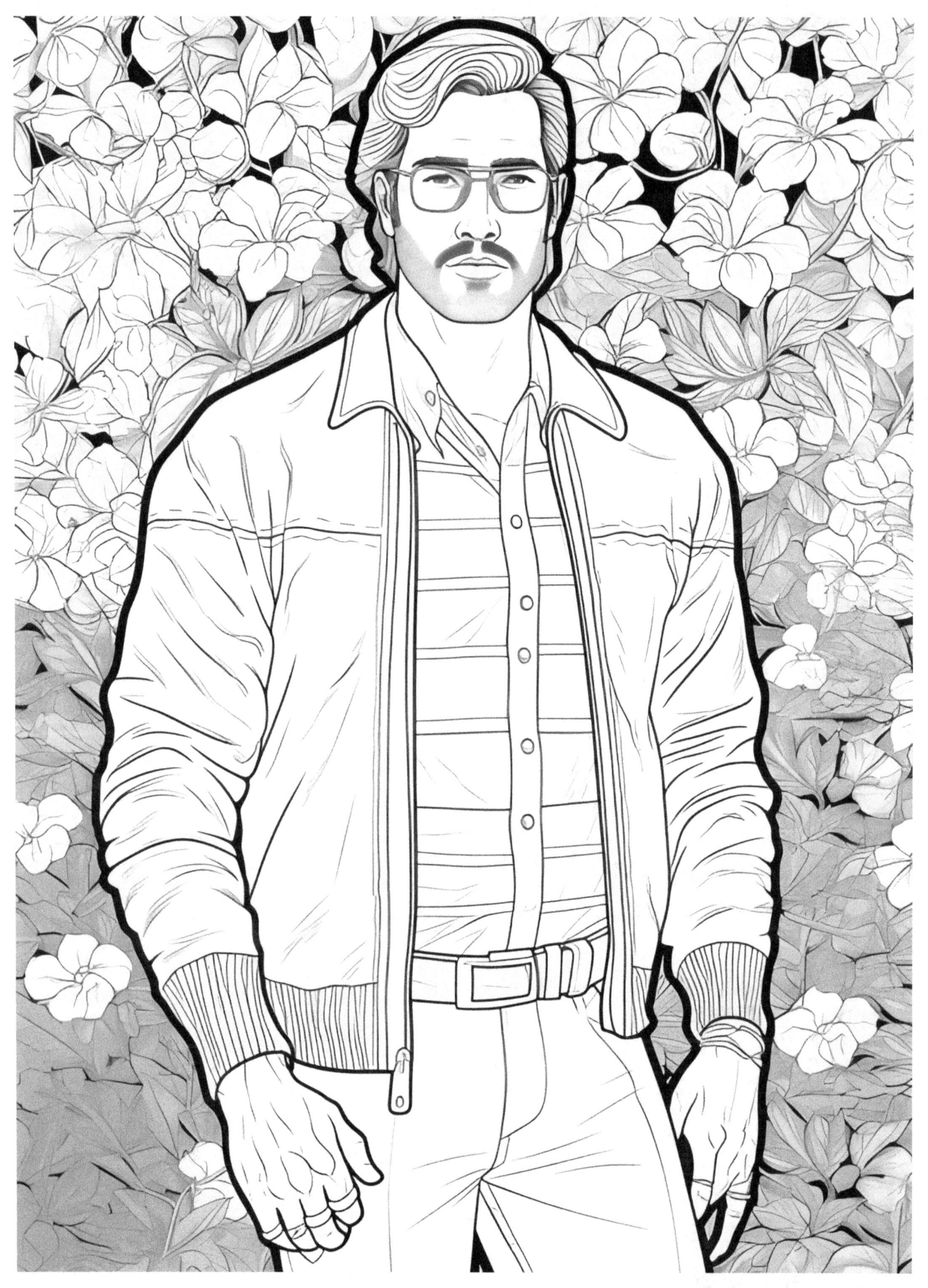

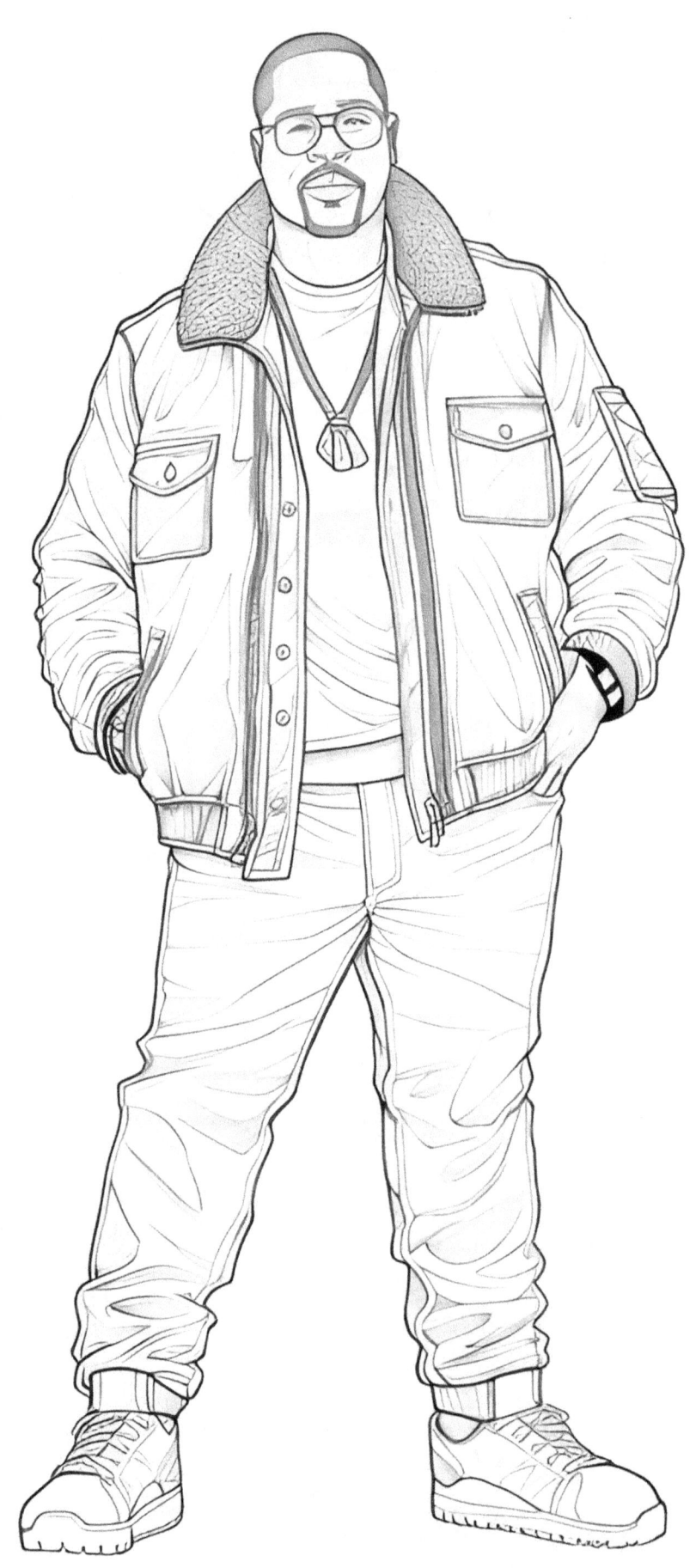

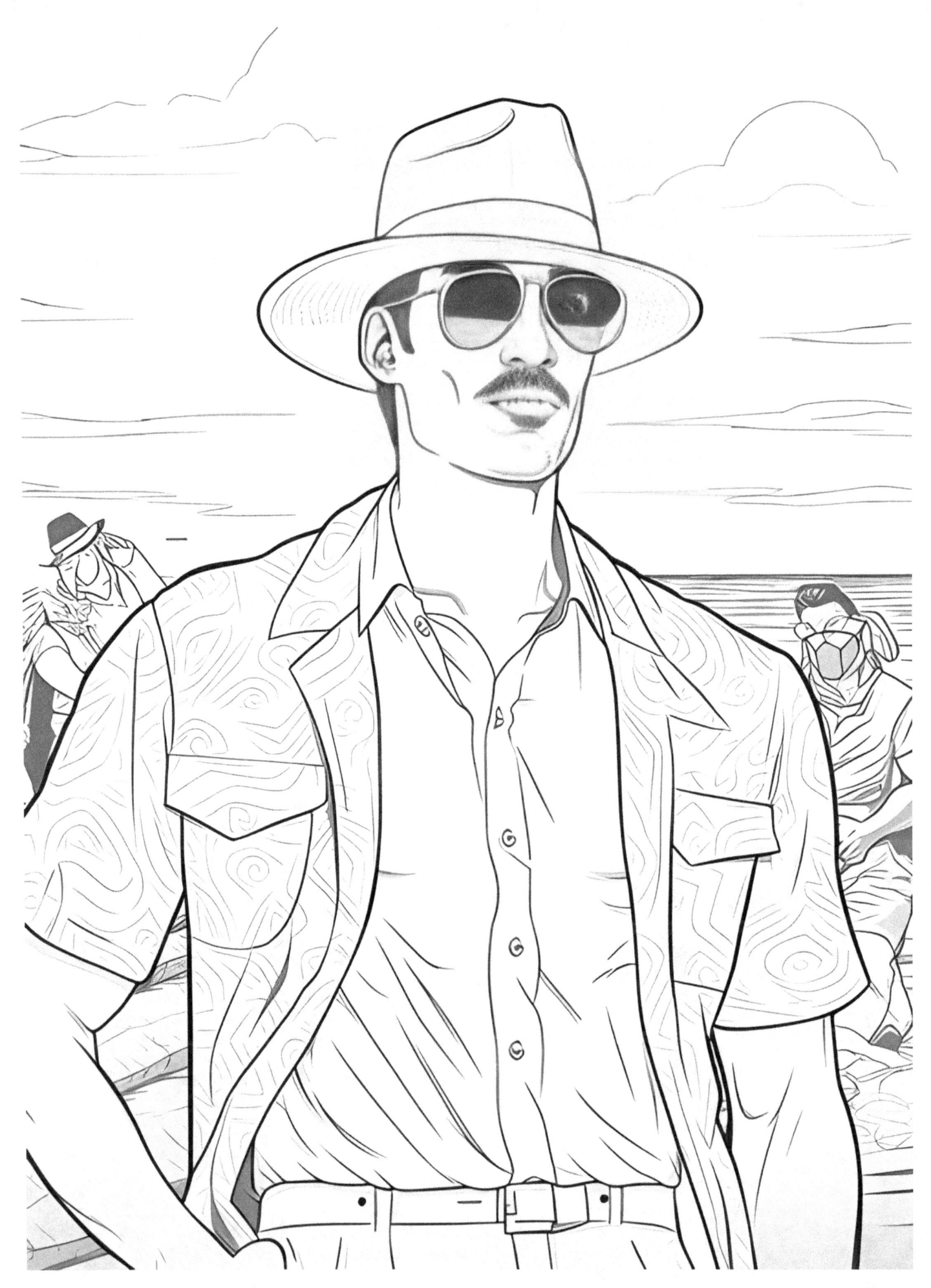

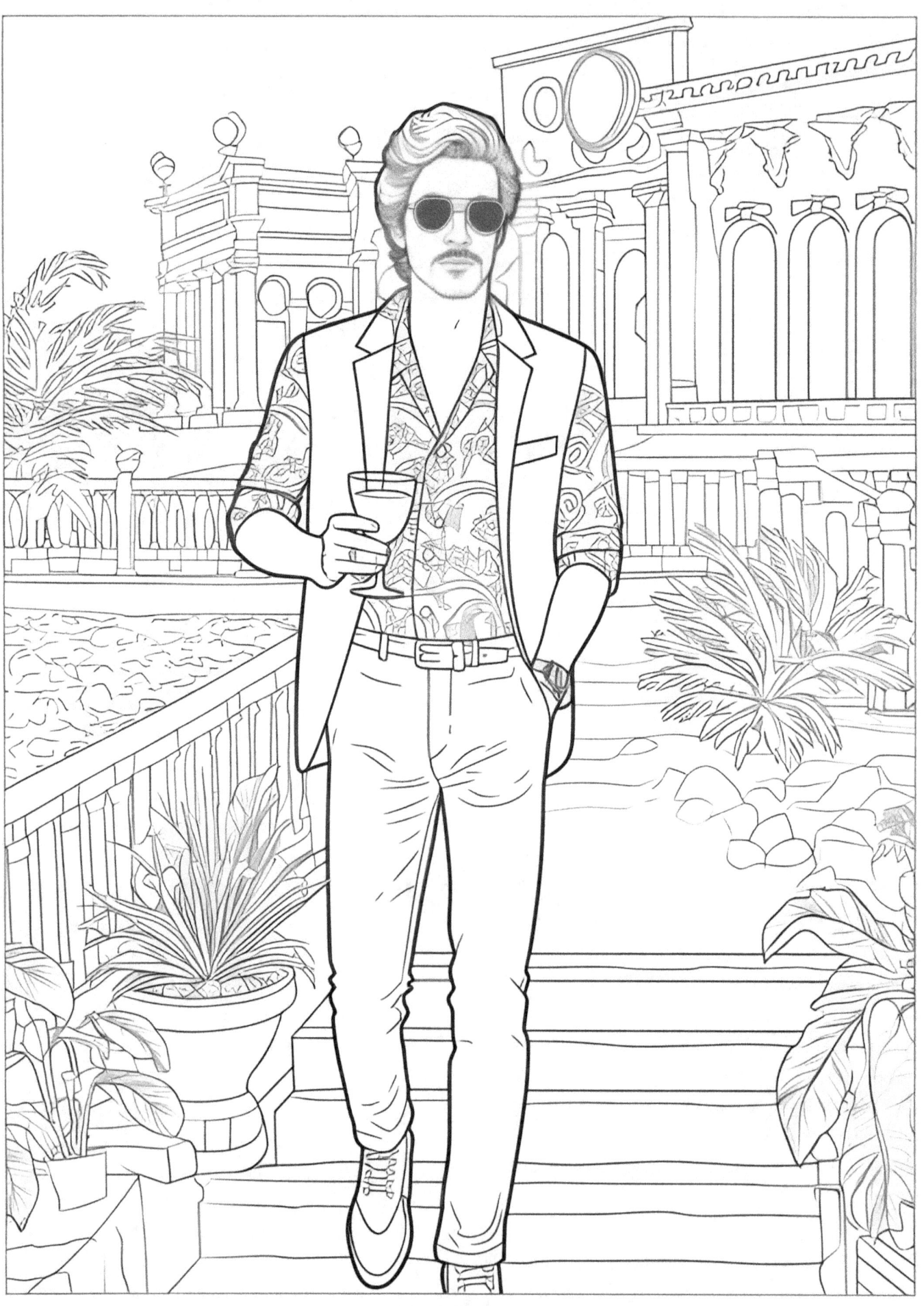

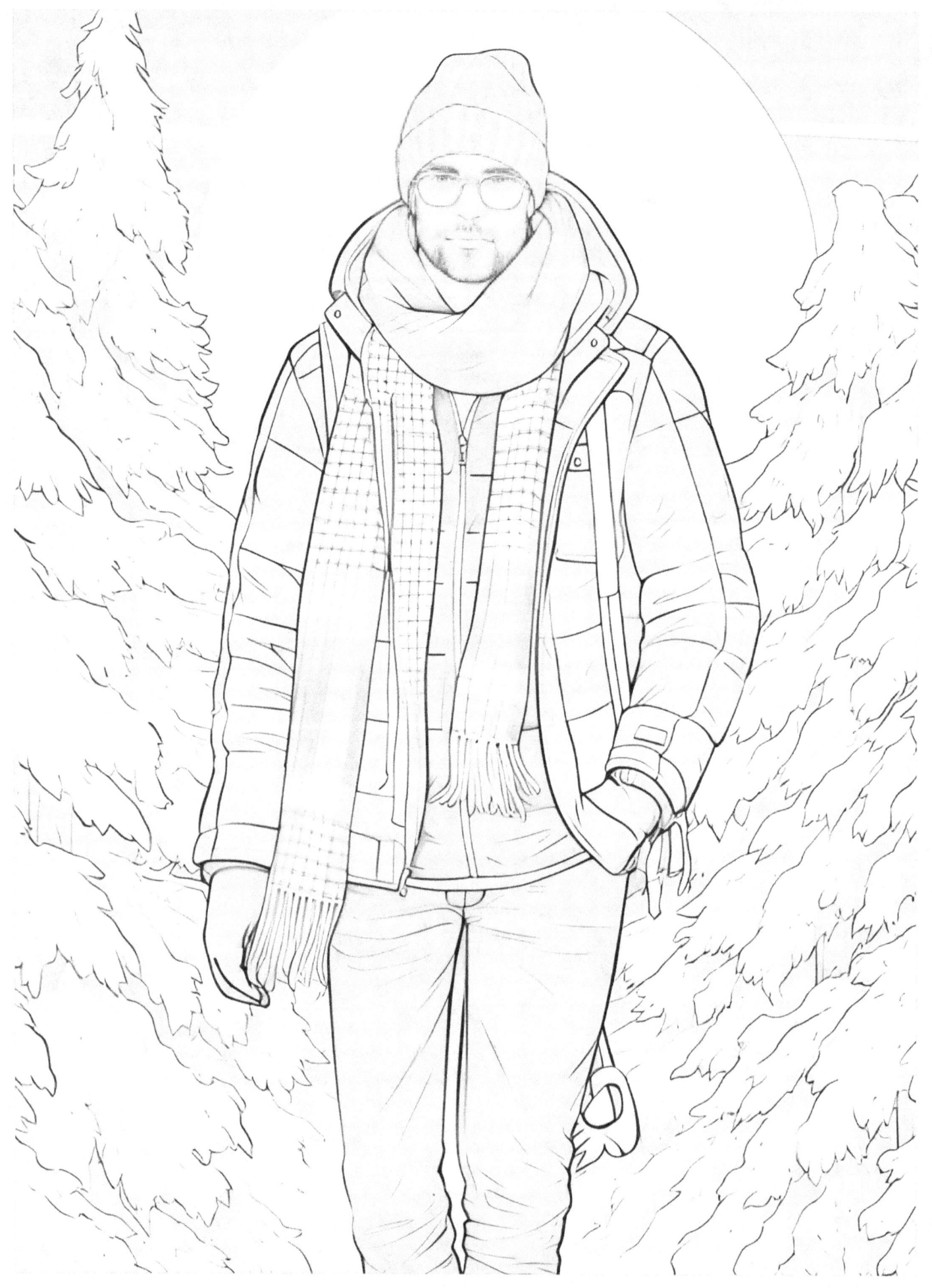

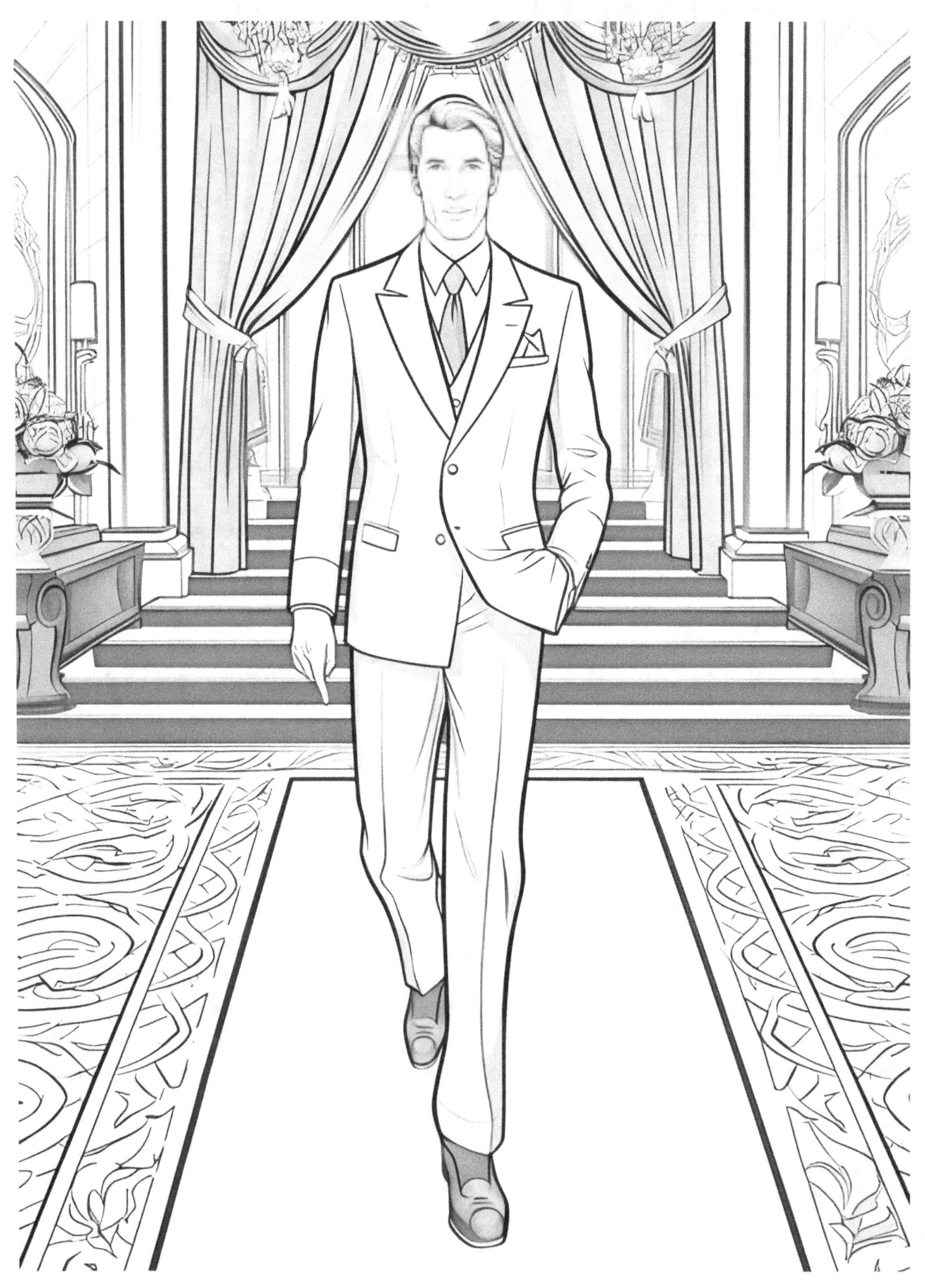

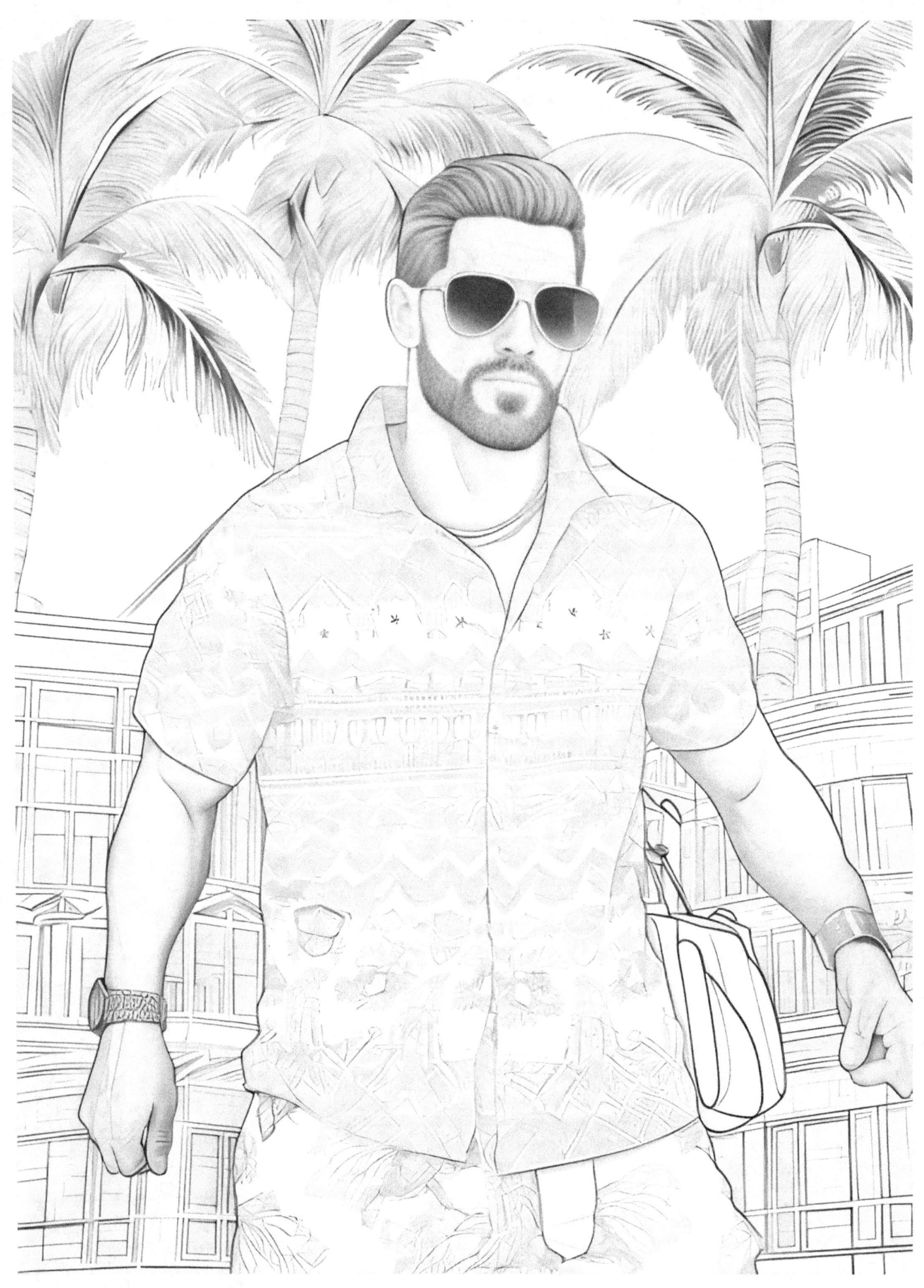

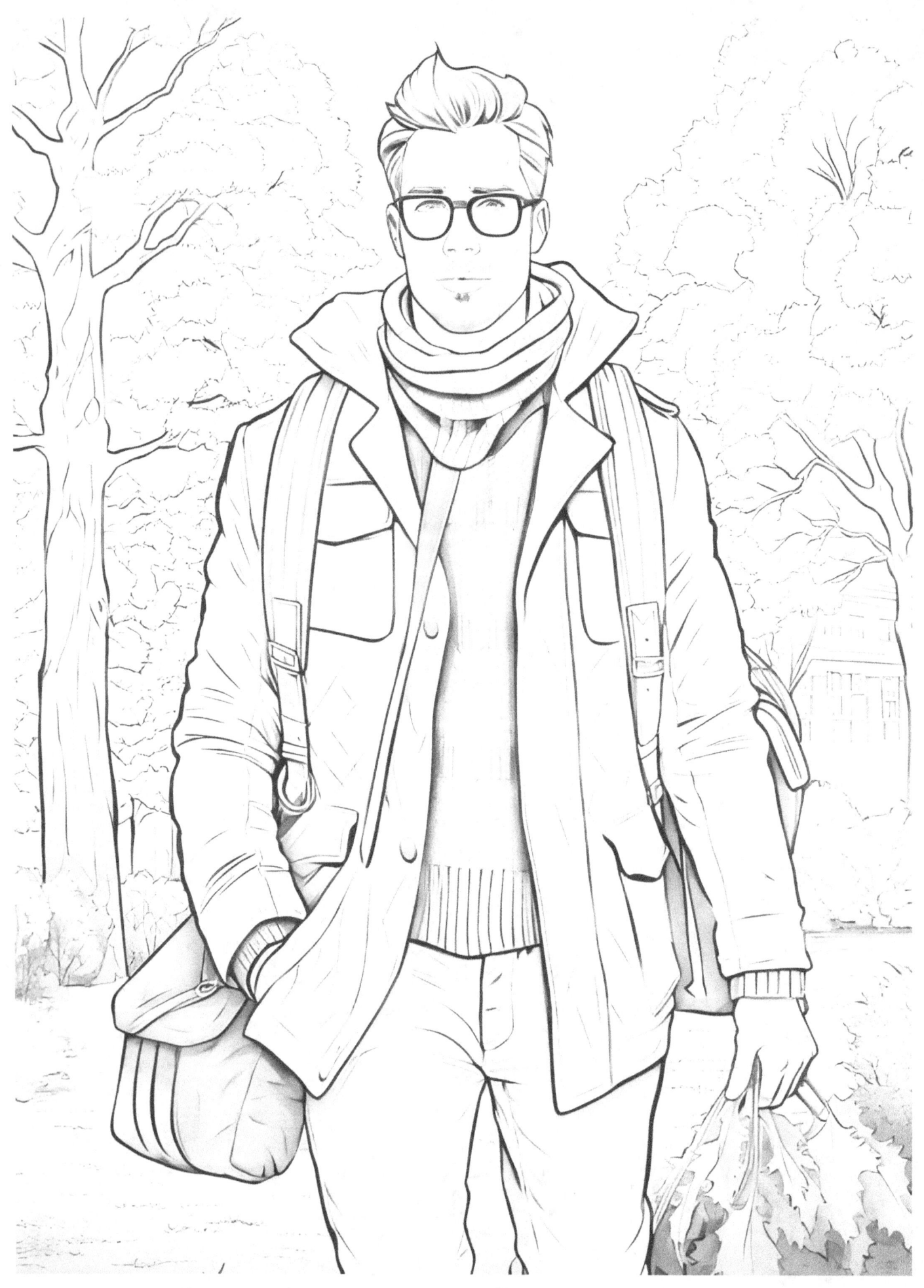

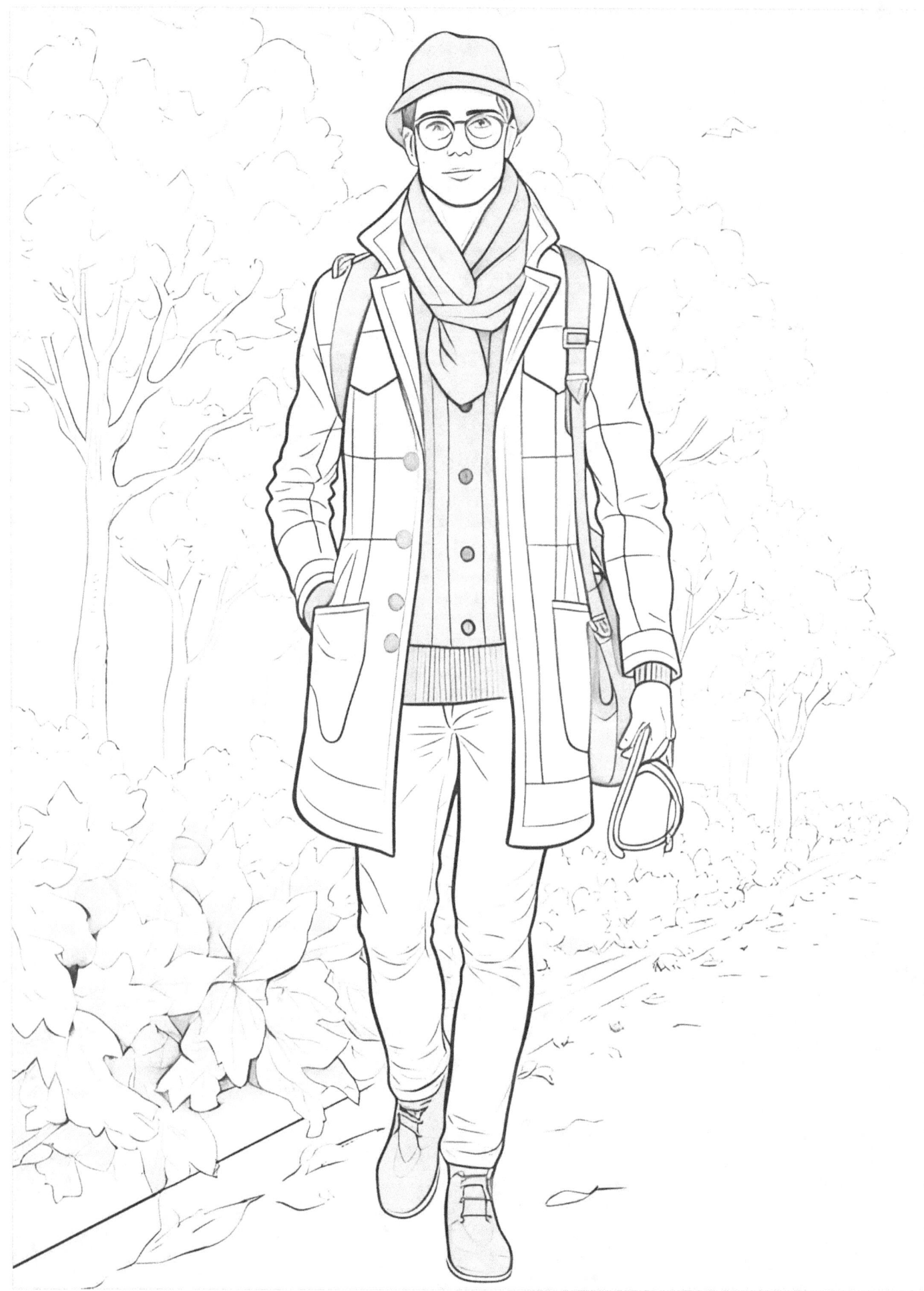

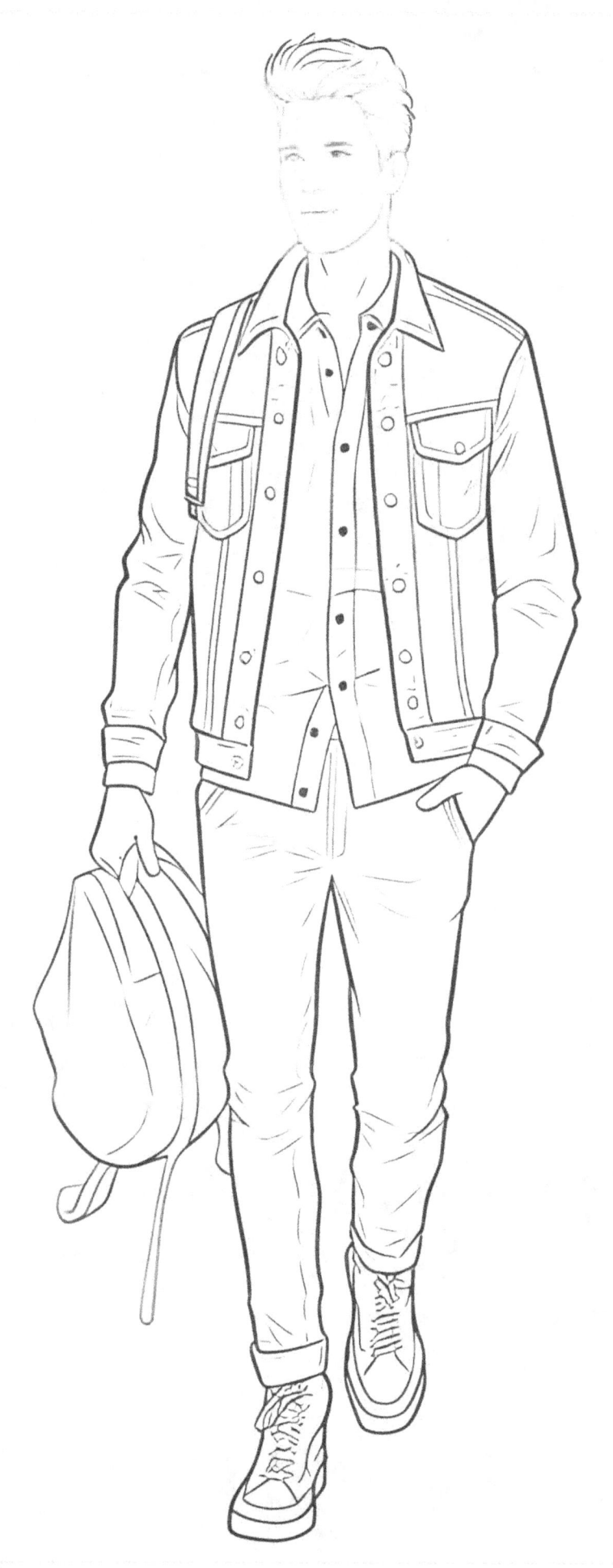

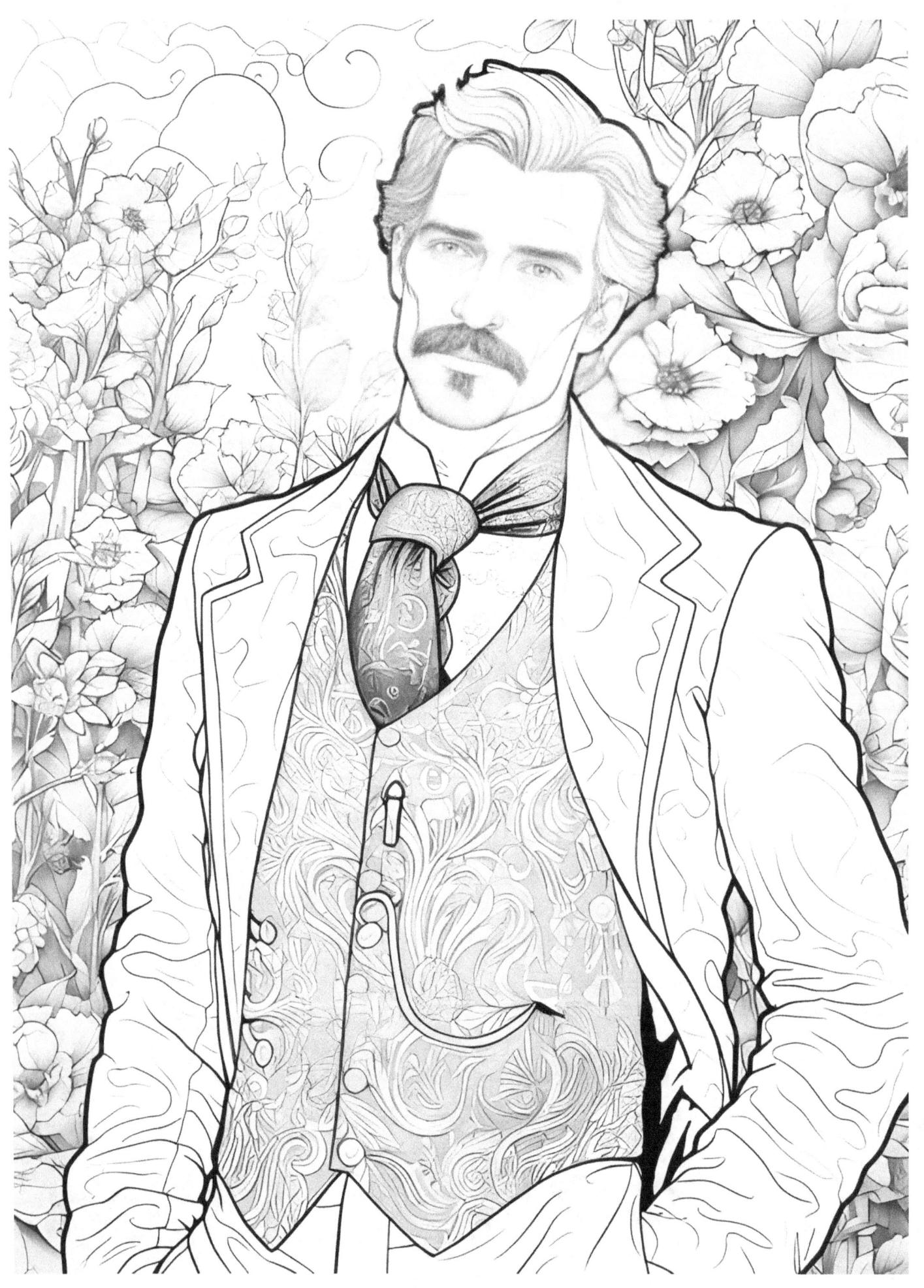

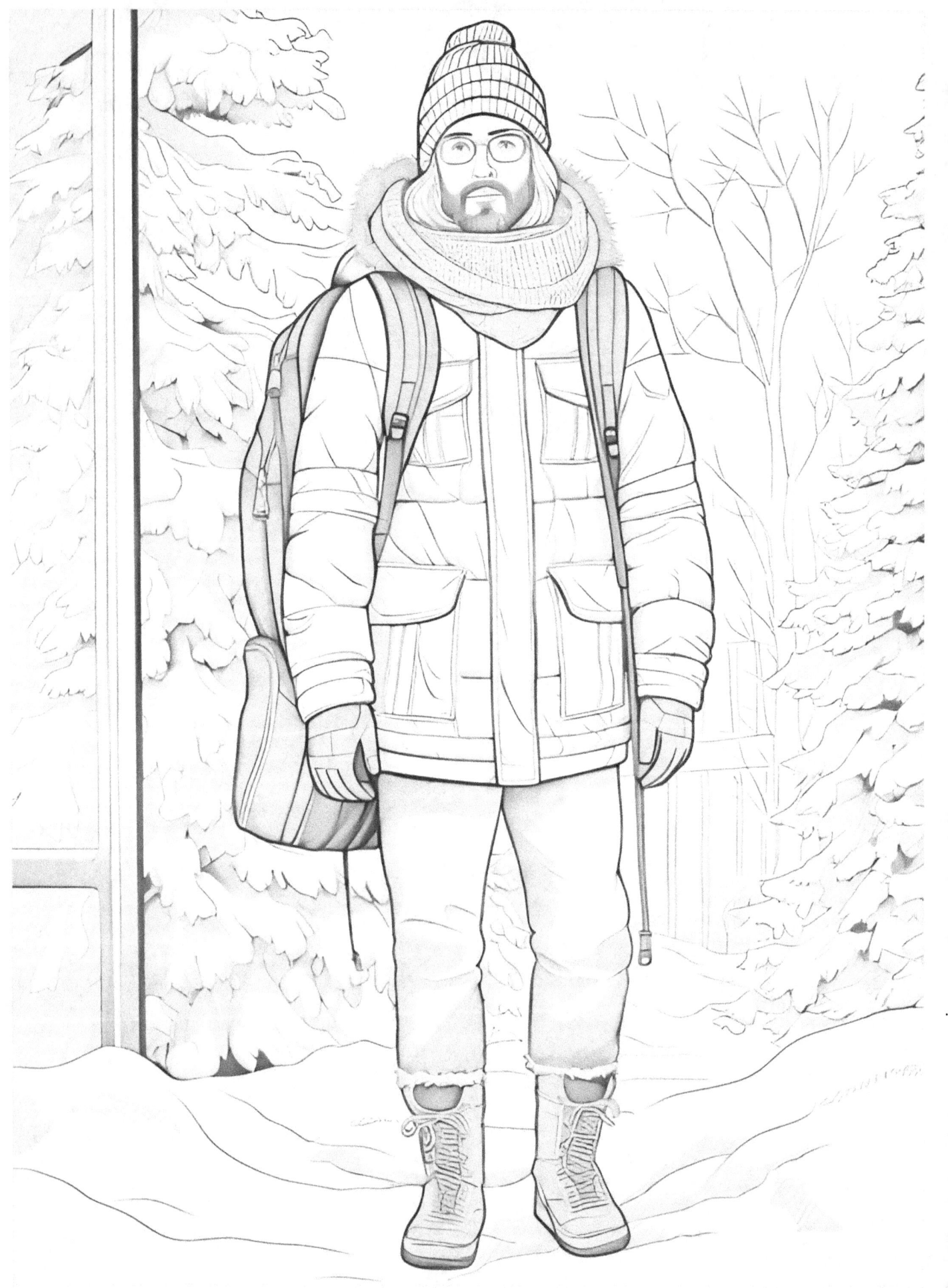

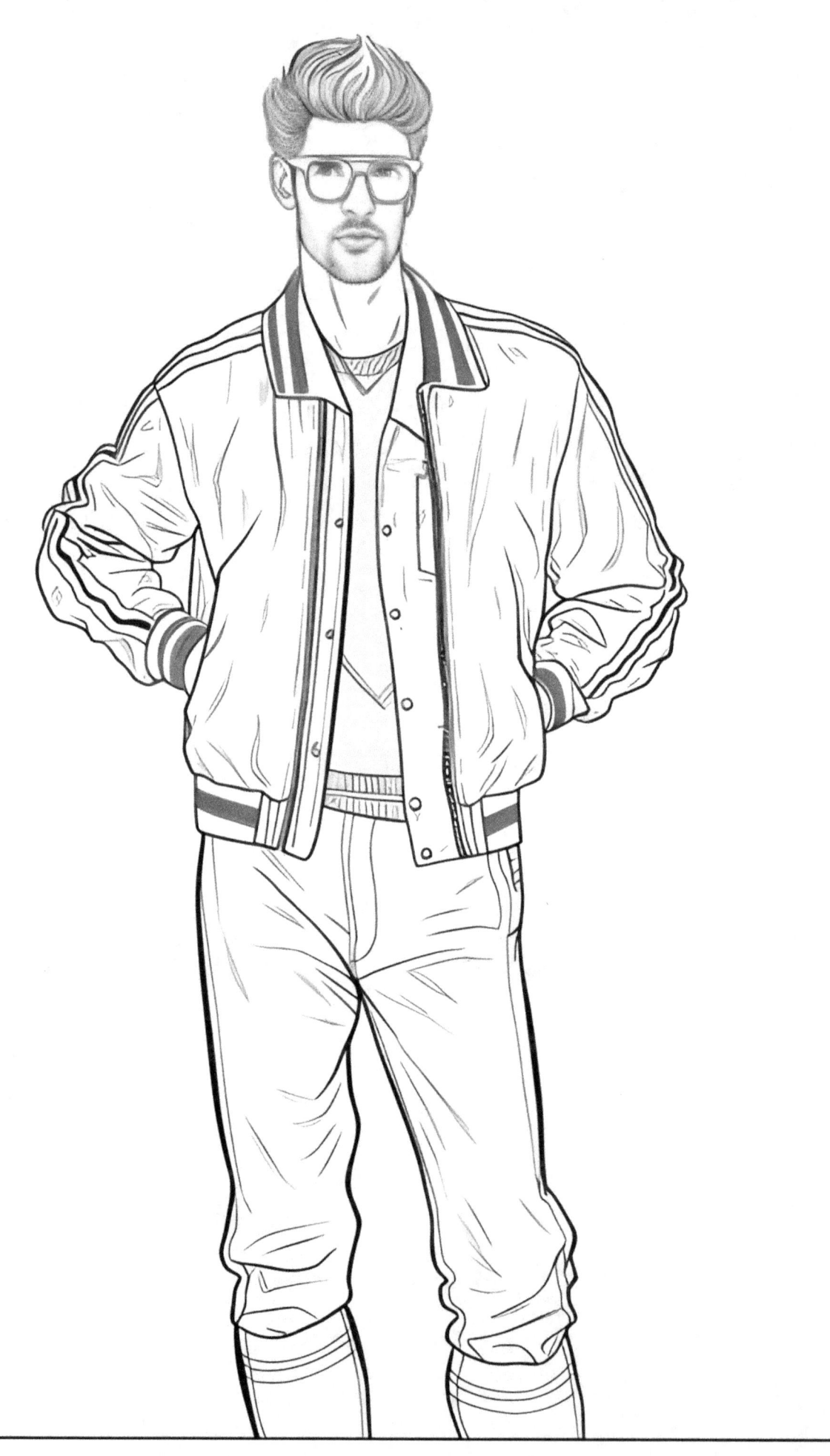

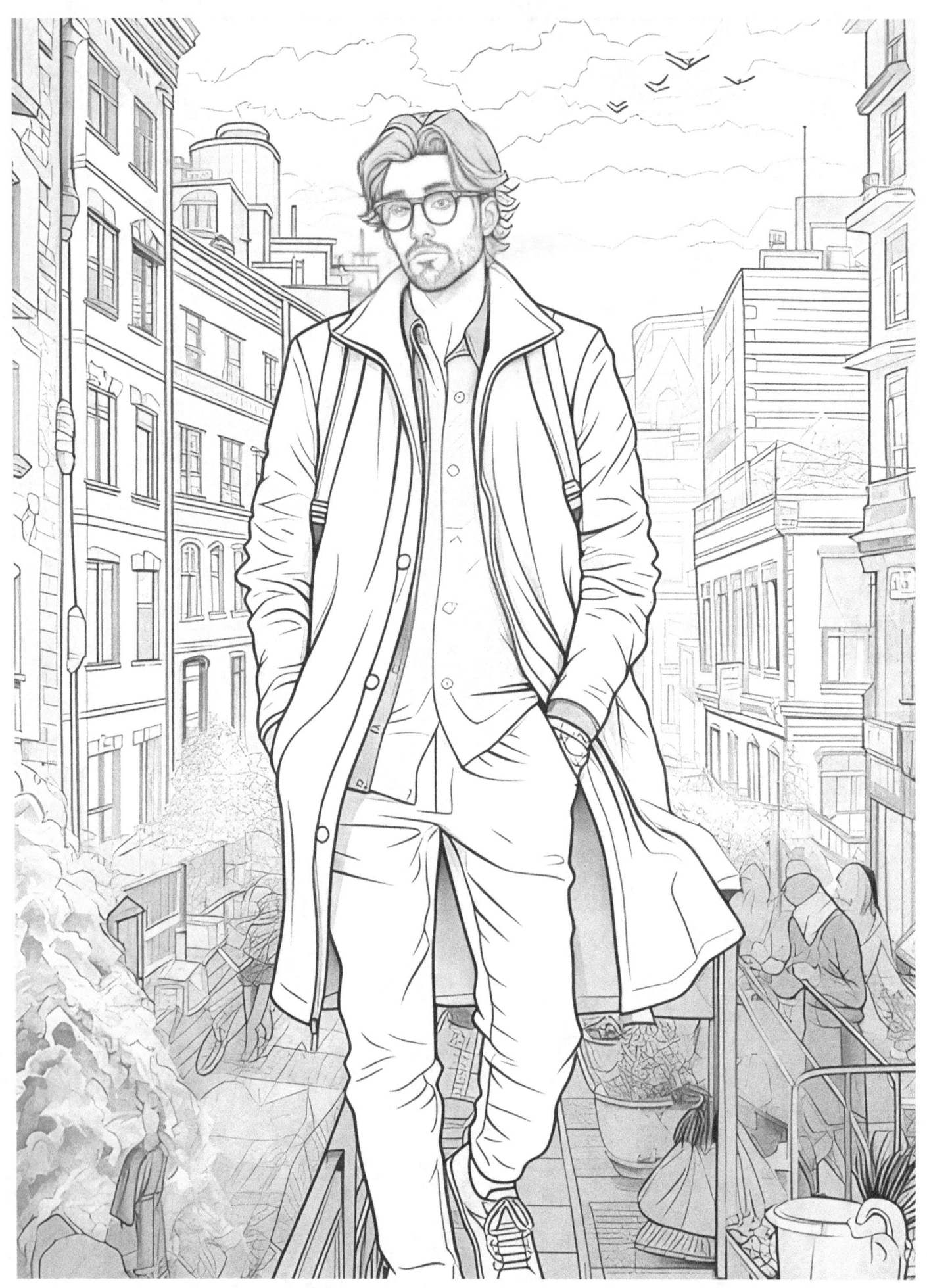

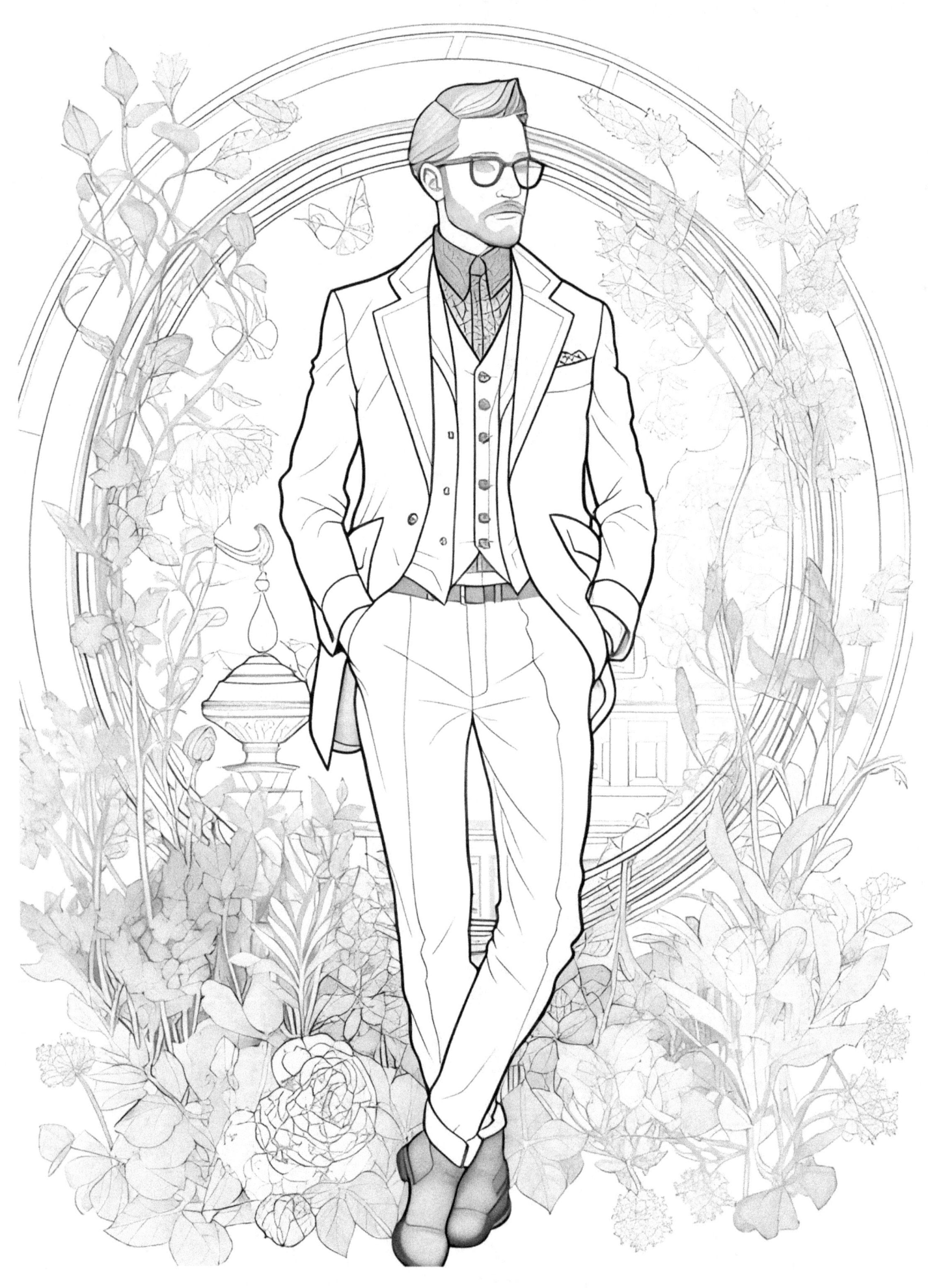

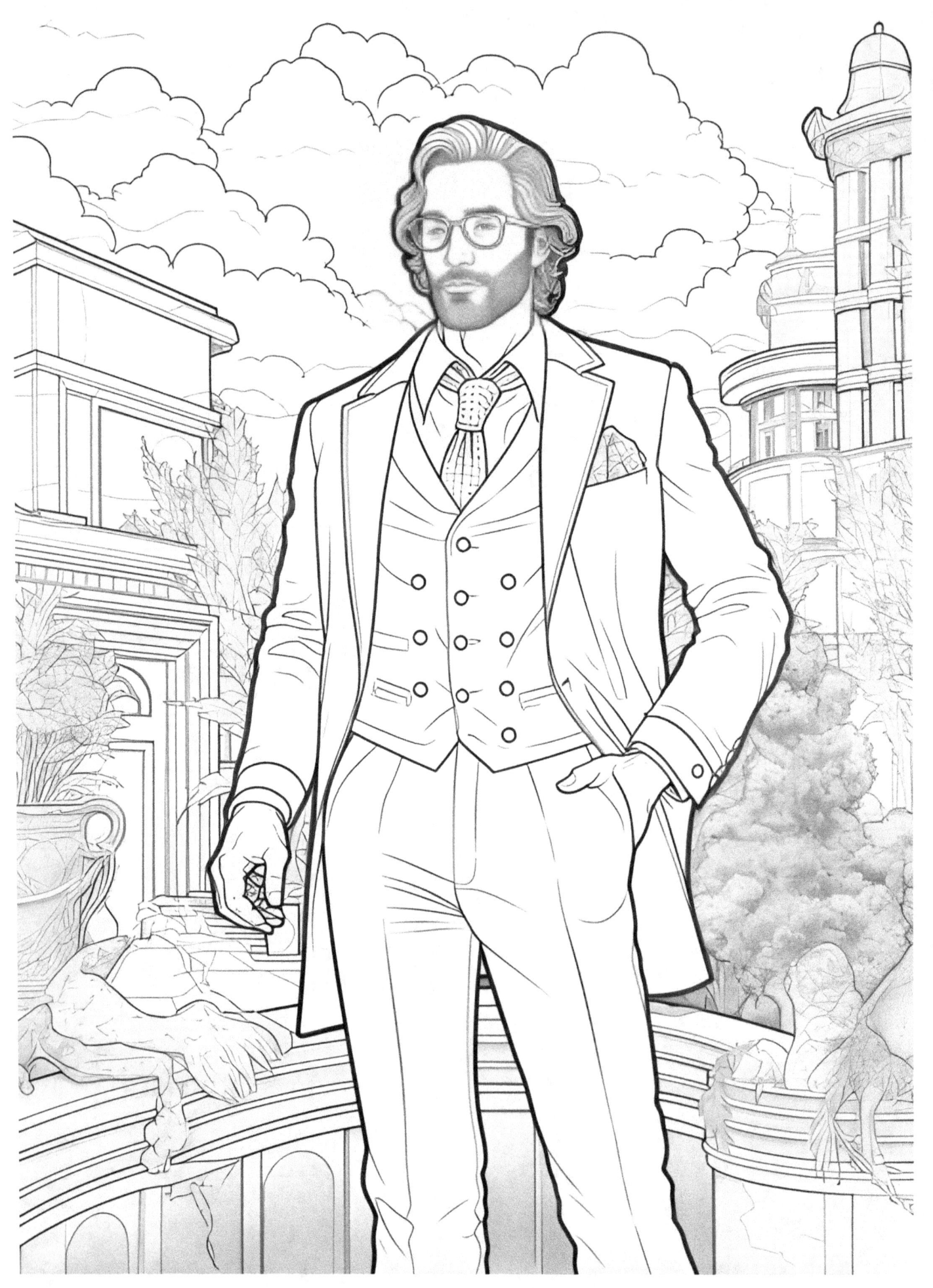

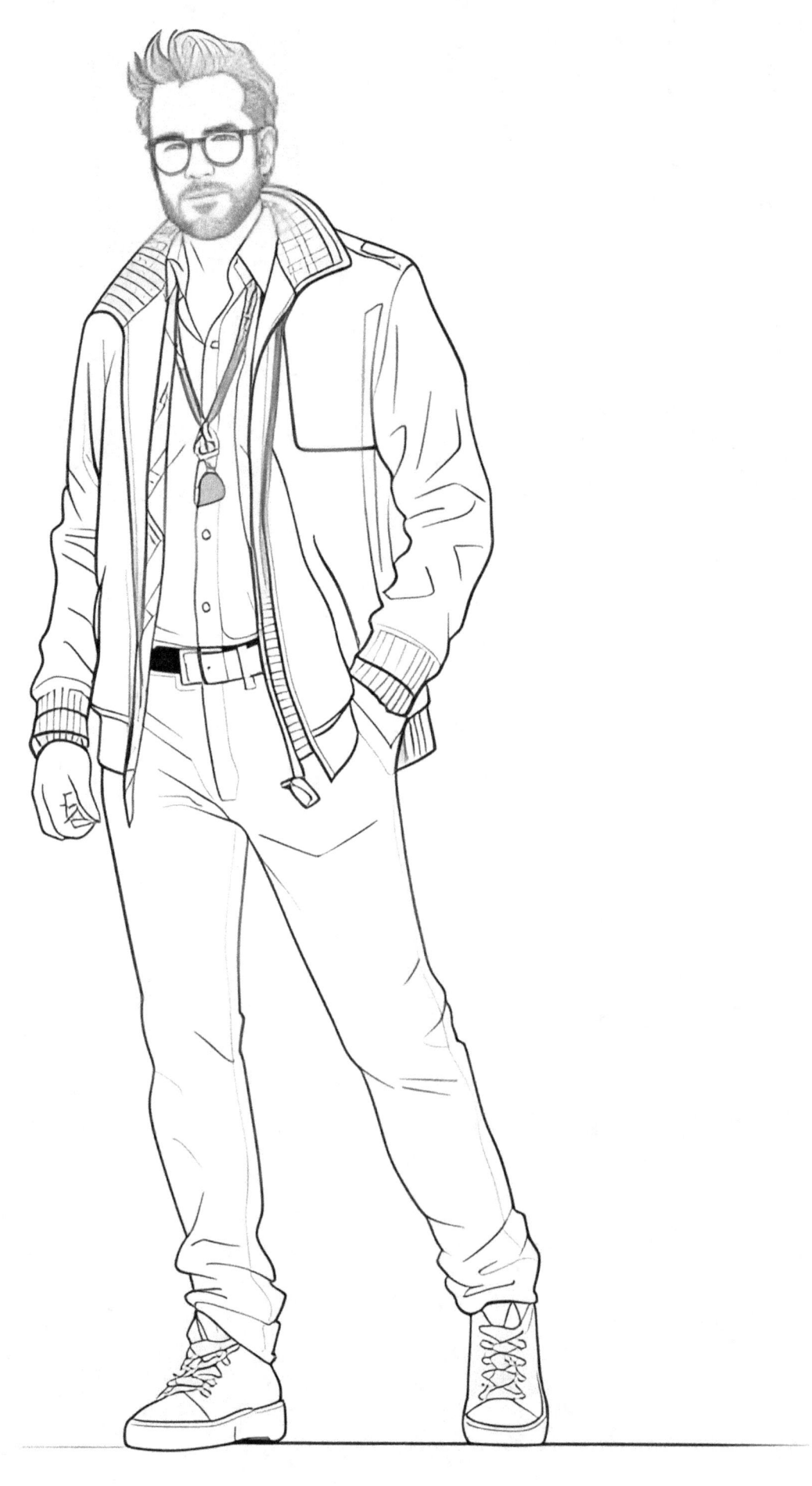

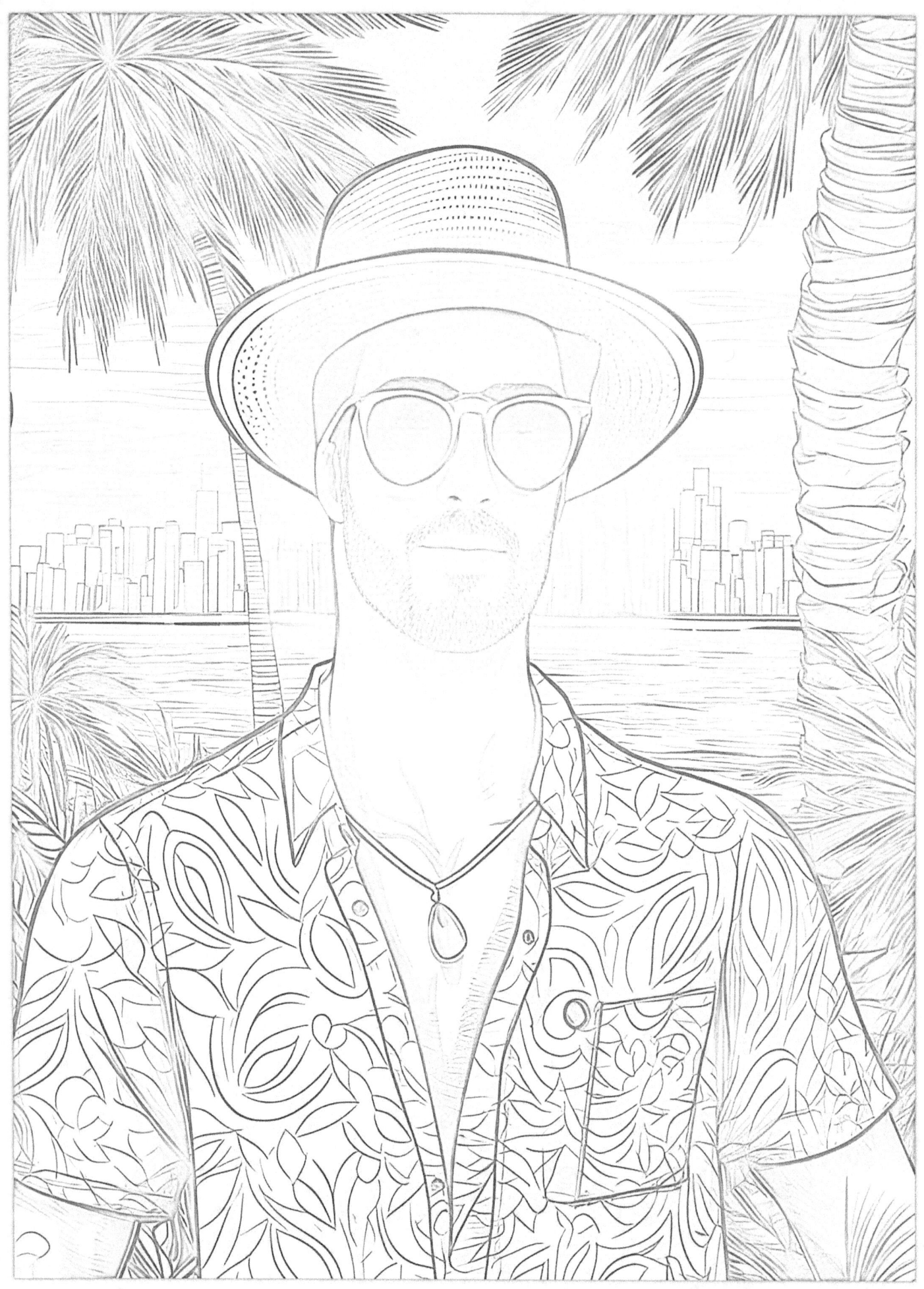

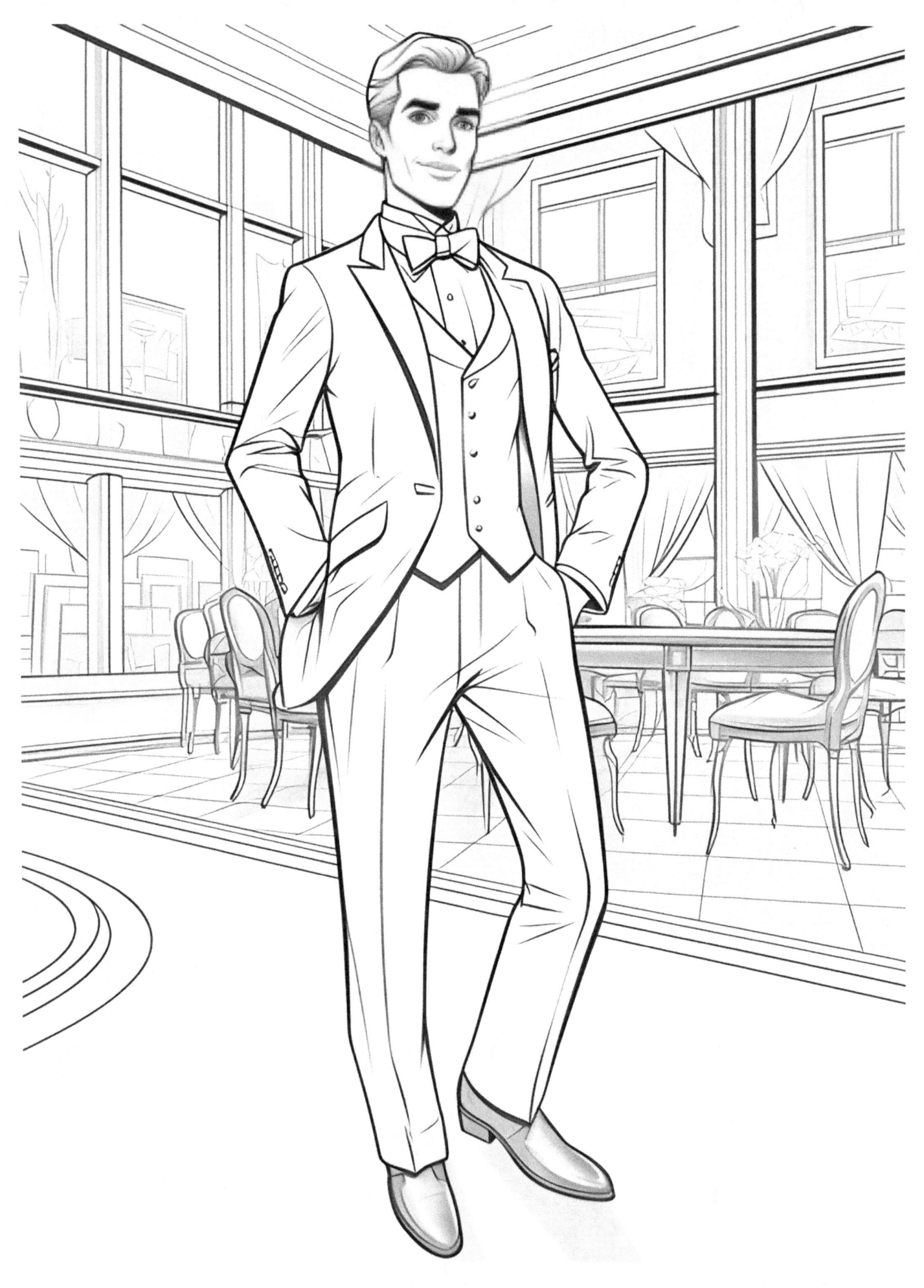

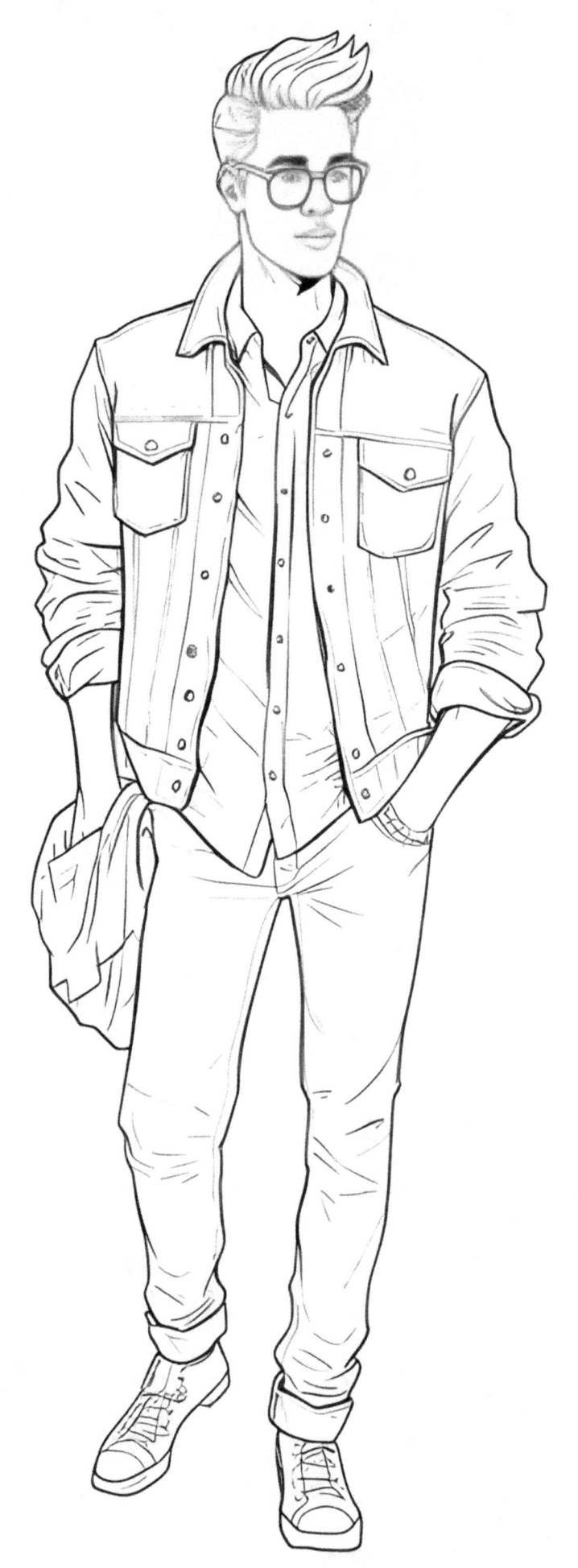

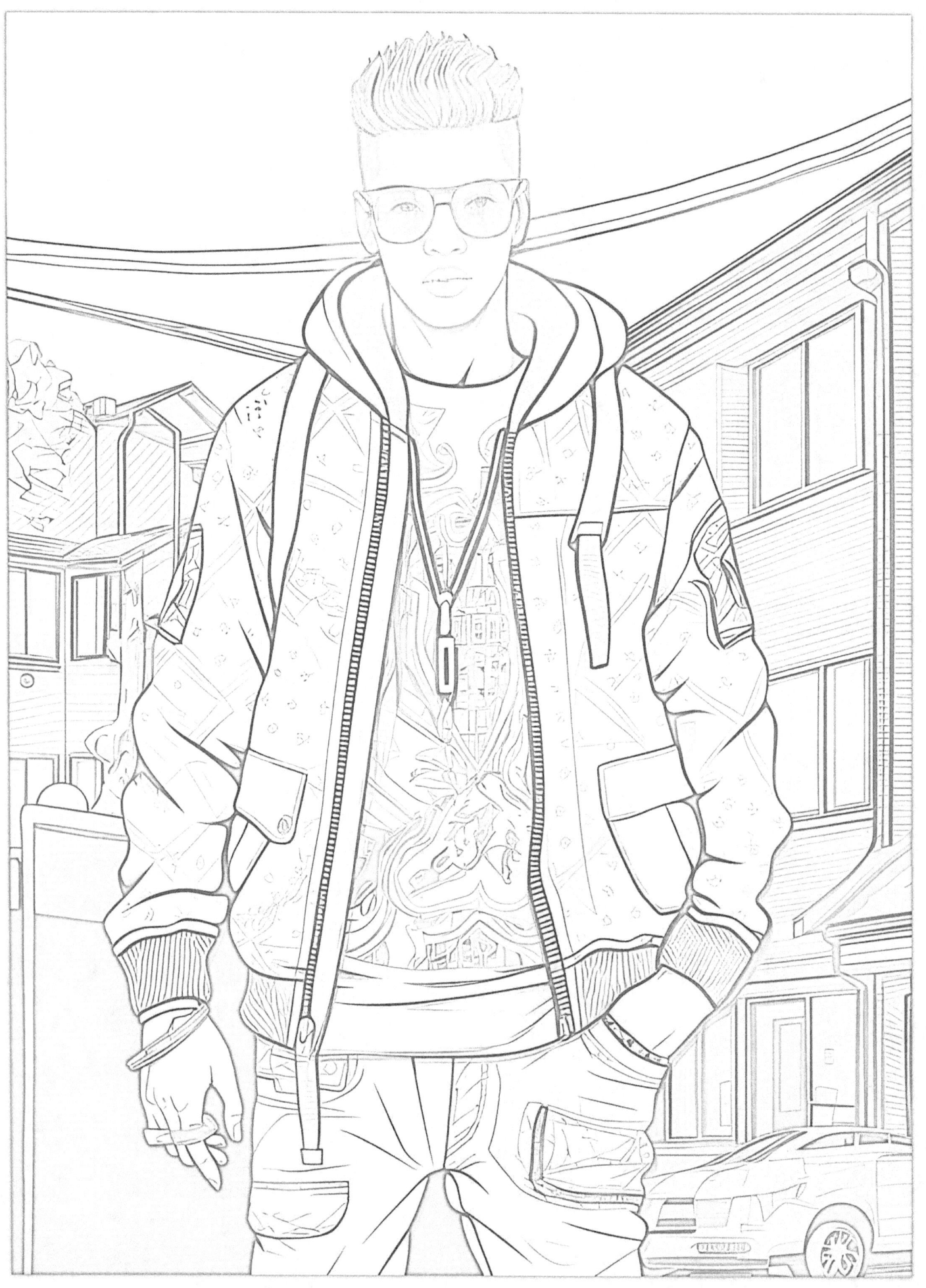

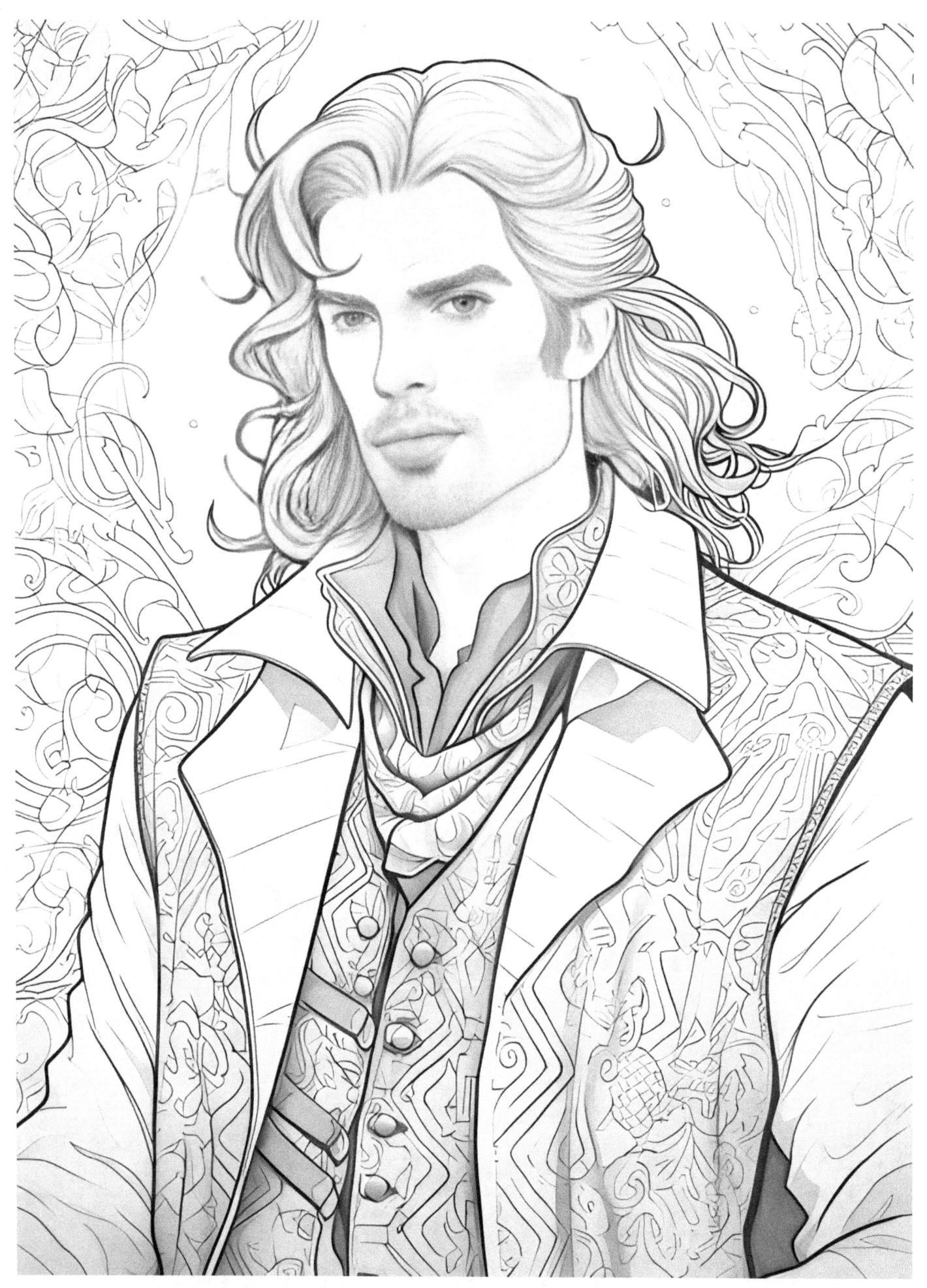

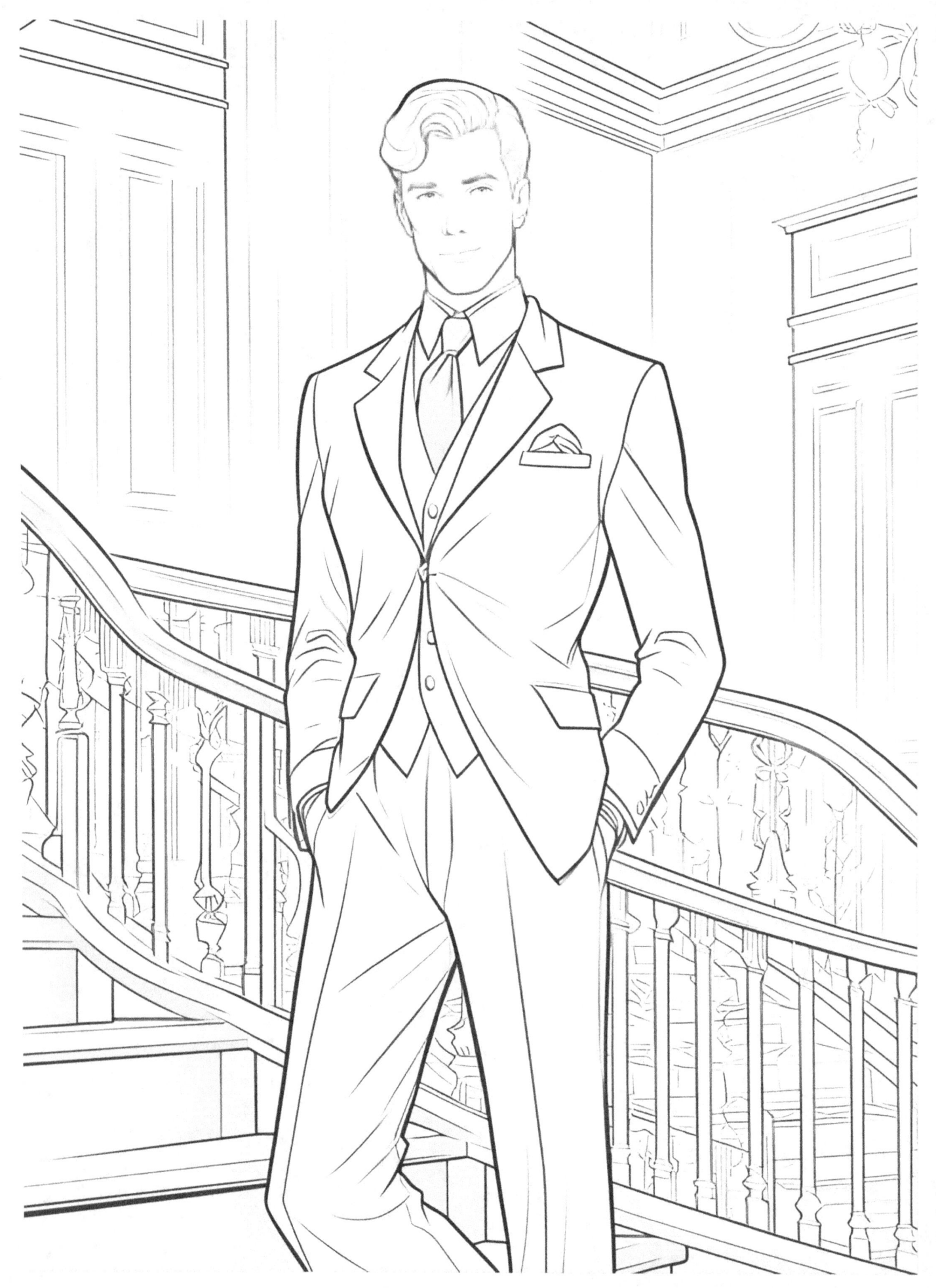

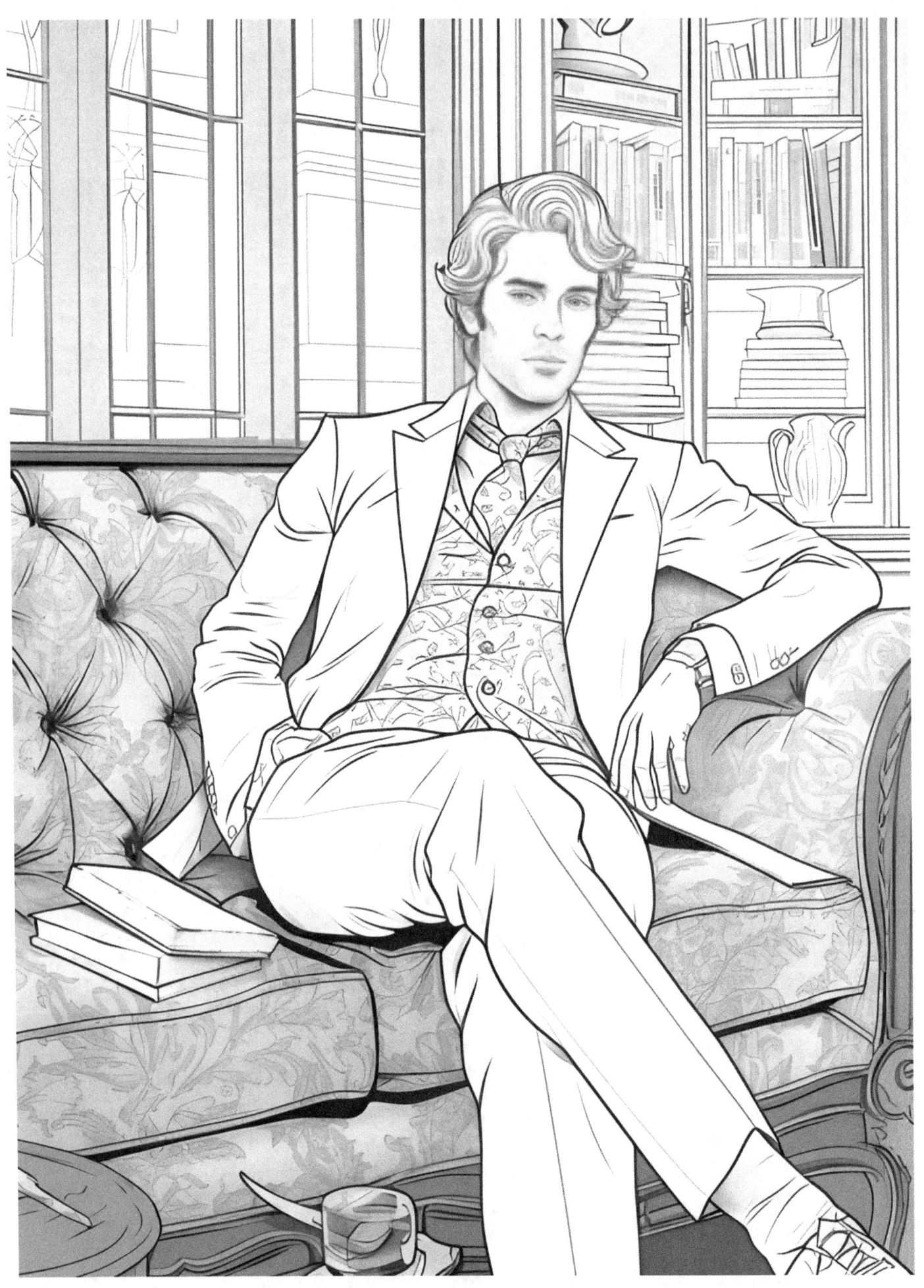

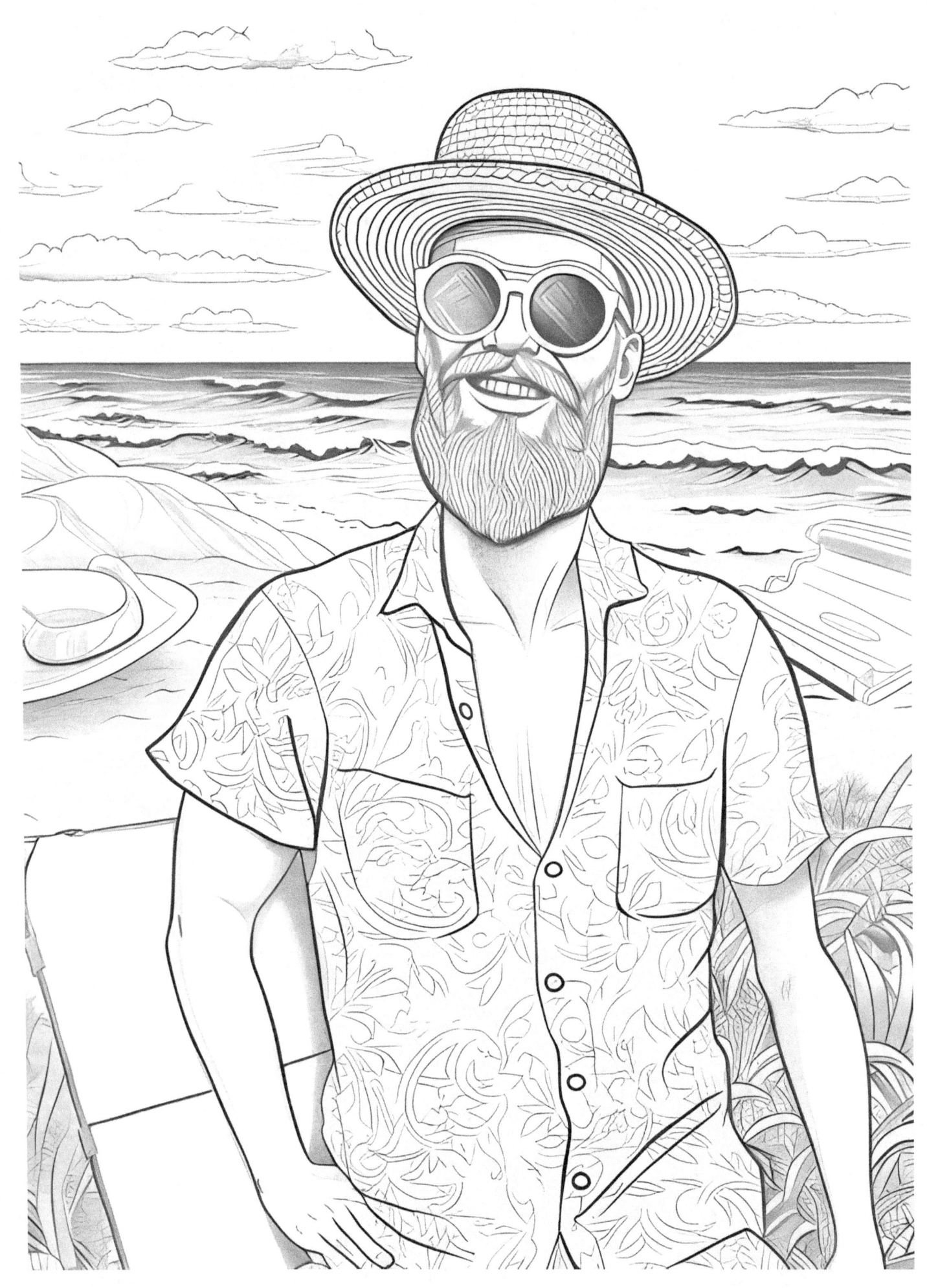

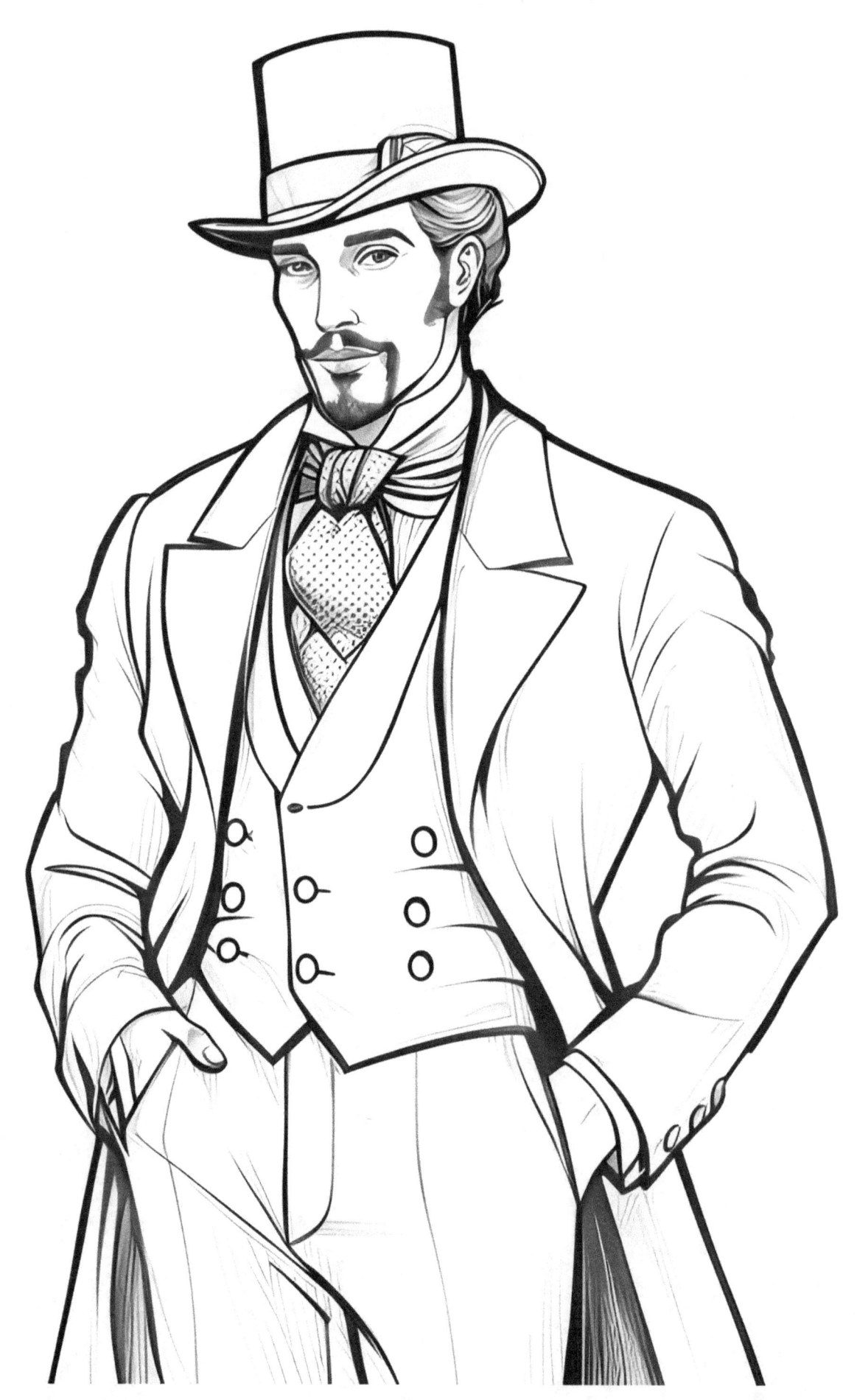

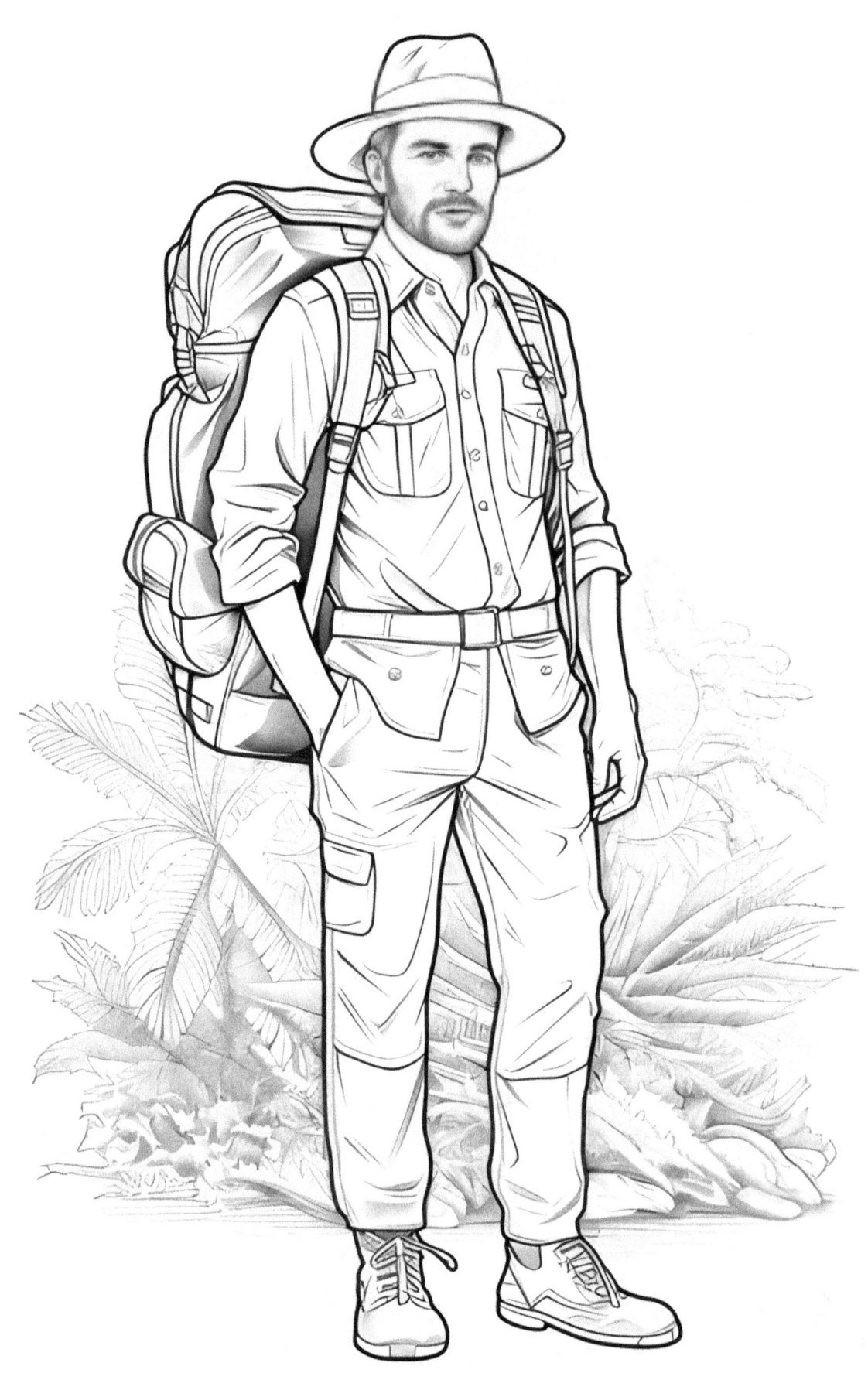

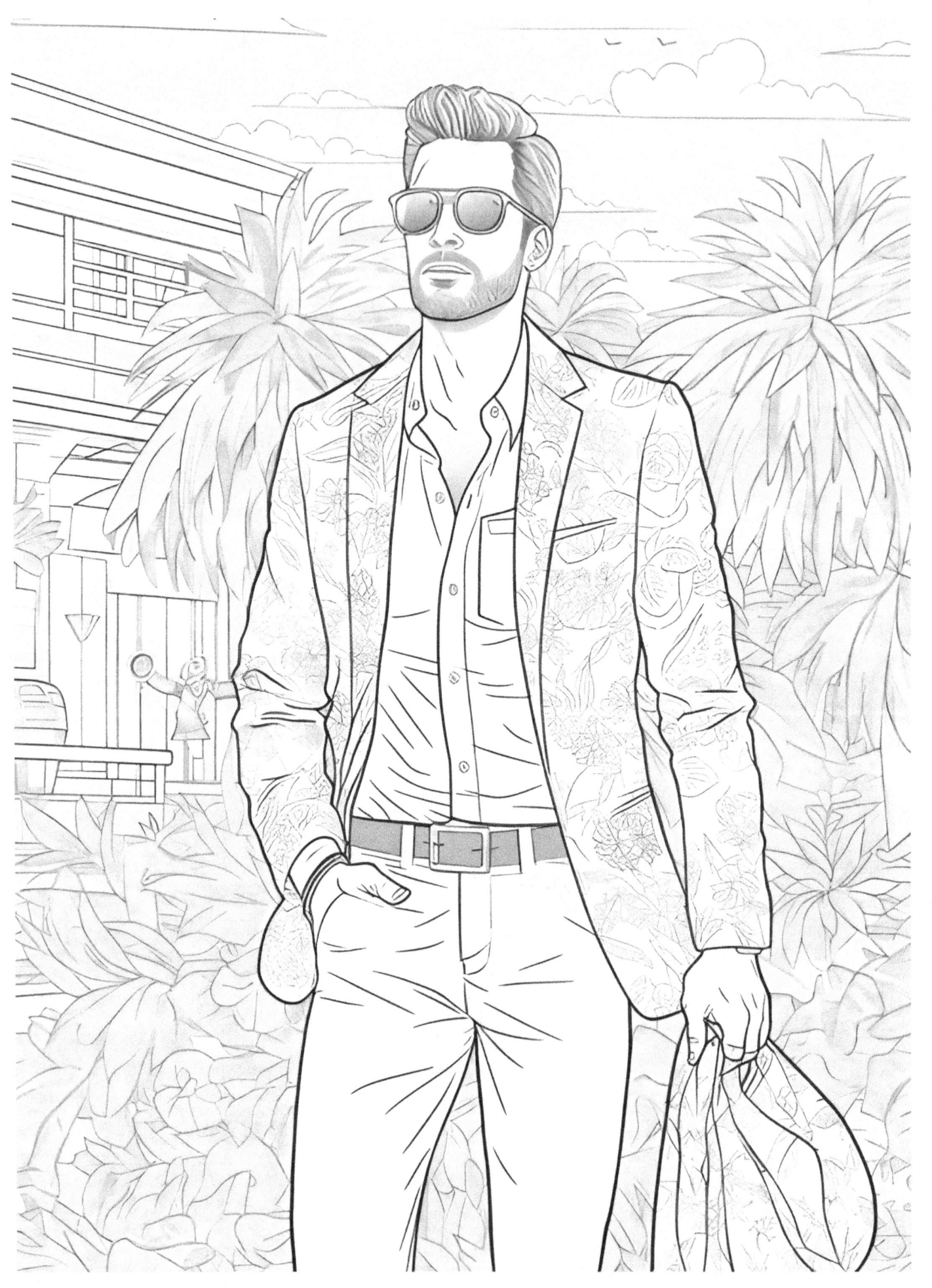